Plaza Suite

Books by Neil Simon

Barefoot in the Park
The Odd Couple
Sweet Charity
Plaza Suite

PLAZA SUITE

Directed on Broadway by Mike Nichols

Neil Simon

Random House · New York

Photographs by courtesy of Martha Swope

Library of Congress Catalog Card Number: 69-16467

Manufactured in the United States of America
by The Haddon Craftsmen, Scranton, Pennsylvania

PLAZA SUITE *was first presented on February 14, 1968, by Saint-Subber at the Plymouth Theatre, New York City, with the following cast:*

(*In order of appearance*)
VISITOR FROM MAMARONECK

A suite in the Plaza Hotel: a late winter afternoon

BELLHOP	Bob Balaban
KAREN NASH	Maureen Stapleton
SAM NASH	George C. Scott
WAITER	Jose Ocasio
JEAN MCCORMACK	Claudette Nevins

VISITOR FROM HOLLYWOOD

The same suite: an early afternoon in spring

WAITER	Jose Ocasio
JESSE KIPLINGER	George C. Scott
MURIEL TATE	Maureen Stapleton

VISITOR FROM FOREST HILLS

The same suite: a Saturday afternoon in June

NORMA HUBLEY	Maureen Stapleton
ROY HUBLEY	George C. Scott
BORDEN EISLER	Bob Balaban
MIMSEY HUBLEY	Claudette Nevins

Directed by Mike Nichols
Scenic Production by Oliver Smith
Lighting by Jean Rosenthal
Costume by Patricia Zipprodt

Visitor from Mamaroneck

A suite at the Plaza Hotel on the seventh floor, over-looking Central Park. The set is divided into two rooms. The room at stage right is the living room. It is a well-appointed room, tastefully furnished with an entrance door at the extreme right and windows that look out over the park. A door leads into the bedroom, which has a large double bed, etc., and a door that leads to the bath-room. The room also contains a large closet.

It is about four in the afternoon in mid-December. The door of the suite opens and a BELLHOP enters and switches on the lights in the living room. He carries one small overnight bag.

KAREN NASH enters behind him. She wears a six-year-old mink coat which could use a bit of restyling, and a pair of galoshes. Underneath she wears an expensive suit which unfortunately looked better on the model in Bendel's than it does on KAREN. KAREN is forty-eight years old, and she makes no bones about it. C'est la vie. She is a pleasant, affable woman who has let weight and age take their natural course. A mink hat is plopped down on her head. She carries a box from Bendel's with her afternoon's purchases and a small bouquet of flowers.

The BELLHOP closes a half-open window in the living room, switches on the lights and puts the bag on the lug-gage tray. KAREN looks around the living room, crosses to the bedroom and puts her packages down on a chair. The BELLHOP goes to the bathroom and turns a light on in there.

KAREN follows him to the bathroom. The BELLHOP

3

*comes out of the bathroom, crosses the living room, opens
the door to leave and hesitates in the doorway.*

BELLHOP   Everything all right, ma'am?

KAREN   Wait a minute, I want to make sure this is the
right room. (*She crosses back into the living room*) I
know this is Suite 719, but was it always 719?

BELLHOP   Yes, ma'am—719.

KAREN   No, you don't understand. I know sometimes
hotels change the numbers around, and this could
have been 723 or 715. And it's very important I get
719.
    (*She returns to the bedroom for the flowers*)

BELLHOP   I'm here two years, it's always been 719.

KAREN   Because you know about 826 at the Savoy-
Plaza?

BELLHOP   No, ma'am.

KAREN   (*Unwrapping the flowers at a table behind the
sofa in the living room*)   Oh, well, they had a famous
murder in 826. Then the next year there was a fire,
and the year after that a husband and a wife com-
mitted suicide. Then no wanted 826. So they turned it
into a linen closet. It's a fact, there is no more 826 at
the Savoy-Plaza.

BELLHOP   There's no more Savoy-Plaza either. They tore
it down two years ago.

KAREN   (*Looks at him incredulously, then goes to look out
the window*)   Oh, my God, look at that. There's no
Savoy-Plaza . . . What's that monstrosity?

4

BELLHOP It's the new General Motors building.

KAREN (*Still looking out the window*) Shows you how often I get into the city. Well, listen, that's what they're doing today. If it's old and it's beautiful, it's not there in the morning . . .

BELLHOP (*Indicating the other windows*) Well, you still have a nice view from here.

KAREN (*Crosses to the other windows and looks out*) Mmmm, for how long? I guarantee you Central Park comes down in five years.

BELLHOP You think so?

KAREN (*Starts to put the flowers in a vase on the sofa table*) I *know* so. Five years from now you'll look out this window and you'll see one little tree and the world's largest A and P.

BELLHOP I don't think I'll be working here five years from now.

KAREN You mean the rumor is true?

BELLHOP What rumor?

KAREN That the Plaza is coming down too!

BELLHOP *This* Plaza?

KAREN (*Puts the vase on the chest between the windows*) I don't want to worry you or anything. It's just a rumor. No one knows for sure . . . But it's definitely coming down.

BELLHOP I didn't hear that.

KAREN (*Crossing to the bedroom, she takes a bag from the luggage rack and puts it on the dresser in front of the bedroom window*) Well, I'm sure they want to keep it quiet from the staff. The story is that they're going to tear down the Plaza and put up a fifty-two-story luxury hotel.

BELLHOP Why? *This* is a luxury hotel.

KAREN Yeah, but it's an *old* luxury hotel. Today it has to be new. Old is no good any more. (*Picks up the phone on the chest in the living room*) Well, all I really care about is tonight.

BELLHOP Yes, ma'am. Is there anything else?

KAREN Oh, wait a minute. (*She puts down the phone, runs to the bedroom for her purse and looks for change*) Don't tell me I don't have any change.

BELLHOP That's all right, ma'am.

KAREN (*Crossing back into the living room*) It's not all right. This is your living. (*Takes out a dollar bill*) Here you are.

BELLHOP (*Taking it*) Thank you very much.

KAREN I'll be very honest with you. I don't usually give dollar tips. But it's my anniversary. So I can be a sport.

BELLHOP (*With his hand on the door. He'd really like to go*) Oh, well, congratulations.

KAREN Thank you, dear. Twenty-four years ago tonight I spent my honeymoon in this room. This *is* 719, isn't it?

BELLHOP Yes, ma'am—719.

KAREN I bet you weren't even born twenty-four years ago, right?

BELLHOP   No, I was born . . .

KAREN   You know what I was? I was twenty-five. You
know what that makes me today? . . . Some old lady.

BELLHOP   Well, you certainly don't look like an old lady.
(*Smiles*) . . . Well . . . have a pleasant stay, ma'am
. . . and happy anniversary.
(*He starts out the door*)

KAREN   Thank you, dear . . . and take my advice. Don't
rush . . . but look around for another job. (*The* BELL-
HOP *nods and exits.* KAREN *crosses to the bedroom and
looks at herself in the full-length mirror on the closet
door. She takes off her hat and puts it on the dresser*)
. . . You are definitely some old lady. (*She crosses to
the phone on the night table next to the bed, takes it
and sits on the bed, still wearing her mink coat*) . . .
Room service, please. (*She groans as she bends over
to take off the galoshes*) . . . Ohhhhh . . . (*Into the
phone*) . . . No, operator. I was groaning to myself . . .
(*Taking off her coat*) Hello, room service? . . . Listen,
room service, this is Mrs. Sam Nash in Suite 719 . . .
I would like a nice cold bottle of champagne . . . That
sounds good, is it French? . . . Fine . . . with two
glasses and a tray of assorted hors d'oeuvres . . . but
listen, room service, I don't want any anchovies . . .
They always give you anchovy patties with the hors
d'oeuvres and my husband doesn't eat anchovies and
I hate them, so don't give me any anchovies . . . Instead of the anchovies, give me some extra smoked
salmon, or you can split them up . . . half smoked
salmon and half caviars . . . That's right. Mrs. Nash.
719 . . . No anchovies . . . (*She hangs up*) They'll
give me anchovies. (*She puts the phone back on the*

night table) Look at that. No more Savoy-Plaza. *(Starts to take off the galoshes again. The telephone rings. There is one in each room. She gets up and picks up the one next to the bed)* Hello . . . *(The phone in the living room rings again. Hastily she hangs up the bedroom phone and rushes to answer it)* Hello? . . . Oh, Sam. Where are you? . . . Good. Come up. I'm here . . . . What room do you think? . . . 719 . . . Remember? 719? Suite 719 . . . That's right! *(She hungs up)* He doesn't remember . . . *(She rushes to the Bendel box and takes out a sheer negligée. She crosses to the mirror on the closet door and looks at herself with the negligée in front of her. She is not completely enchanted. The telephone rings. She puts down the negligée and rushes to the living room to answer it)* Hello . . . *(The phone in the bedroom rings again. She hastily hangs up the living room phone and rushes to answer it)* Hello? . . . Oh, hello, Miss McCormack. . . . No, he's not, dear. He's on his way up. Yes, I will . . . It's not important, is it? . . . Well, he seemed so tired lately, I was hoping he wouldn't have to think about work tonight. *(Glancing down at her feet)* . . . Oh, my God, I still have my galoshes on . . . All right, I'll tell him to call. Yes, when he comes in. Good-by. *(She hangs up and quickly bends over in an effort to remove her galoshes. She is having difficulty. The doorbell rings)* . . . Oh, damn it. *(Calls out)* Just a minute! *(The doorbell rings again. She is having much trouble with the right galosh)* . . . You had to wear galoshes today, right? *(She pulls her right galosh off but her shoe remains in it. The doorbell rings impatiently)* Oh, for God's sakes . . . *(She tries to pull her shoe out of the galosh but it is imbedded in there)* All right, all right, I'm coming *(She throws down the galosh with the shoe still in one galosh and her stockinged foot. She crosses into the living room)* Look at this, my twenty-fourth anniversary. *(She "limps" to the door and opens it.* SAM NASH *stands there.* SAM *has just turned fifty but has made every effort to conceal it. He is trim, impeccably neat. His clothes are well tailored, although a bit on the junior-executive side. He carries an attaché case, a fine leather Gucci product. Everything about* SAM *is measured, efficient, economic. She smiles warmly)* Hello, Sam.

> *(*SAM *walks brusquely past her, surveying the room)*

SAM   An hour and fifteen minutes I was in the god-damned dentist's chair . . .
> *(He puts down his attaché case on the chair downstage of the door to the bedroom, and takes off his coat)*

KAREN *(Closes the door, still warmly)*   How do you feel, Sam?

SAM   Between his lousy dirty jokes and WQXR-FM, I got some headache. *(He crosses to the mirror over the chest in the living room and looks at his teeth)* Did anyone call?

KAREN   Sam, do you remember this room?
> *(Moving to him)*

SAM *(Still examining his teeth)*   Well, two more caps and I'm through. *(He turns, baring his teeth at her)* What do you think?

KAREN *(Put her hands in front of her eyes to shield the glare)*   Ooh, dazzling!

SAM   You don't think they're too white, do you? *(Turns*

9

and looks in the mirror again) Do they look too white to you?

KAREN No, no. Perfect. Very nice with the blue shirt.

SAM *(Still looking)* These don't stain, you know. A hundred years from now when I'm dead and buried, they'll be the same color.

KAREN Oh, good. You'll look wonderful. You don't remember this room, do you?

SAM *(Looks at his watch)* Four thirty already? The meeting must be over . . . Didn't anyone call?
(Takes his coat and attaché case into the bedroom, putting the coat on the chest and the case on the bed)

KAREN Miss McCormack, from the office . . . She wants you to call back.

SAM *(Looks at her, annoyed)* Why didn't you tell me?

KAREN We were busy talking about your white teeth. Happy anniversary, Sam.
(Picks up a vase and crosses to the bedroom)

SAM *(Not hearing her, into the phone)* Judson 6-5900 . . . What did you say? *(Sees her limp into the bedroom)* What's the matter with your leg?

KAREN *(Limps into the bathroom)* One is shorter than the other. Didn't you ever notice that? I've had it for years.

SAM *(Into the phone)* Lorraine? Mr. Nash. Let me have Miss McCormack, please. *(SAM looks at himself in the closet mirror)* . . . Well, that kills my barber's appointment today. Oh, could I use five minutes under the sun lamp. (*Into the phone.* KAREN *begins to sing in the bathroom*) Miss McCormack? Did Henderson call? . . . Did he send the contracts? (*Places his hand over his ear to shut out* KAREN's *singing*) . . . What about Nizer? . . . I see . . . (*He quickly takes a note pad from the night table and places it on the attaché case on the bed in front of him. He can't find a pencil. He snaps his fingers at* KAREN. *Still into the phone*) What does it look like? . . . Ah huh . . . ah huh . . . (*He snaps his fingers at* KAREN *again*) A pencil . . . pencil . . . (KAREN, *rushing in from the bathroom, searches through the night tables on both sides of the bed and dresser.* SAM *is still on the phone*) Very good. All right, give me the figures. (*He nods into the phone.* KAREN *still can't find a pencil. She limps hurriedly over to her purse on the sofa table in the living room.* SAM, *into the phone*) . . . It sounds right, but I've got to go over the estimates . . . Tomorrow morning? That doesn't give us much time . . . Wait a minute, give me those figures again . . . (*He puts his hand over the phone, and whispers angrily*) Karen, for God's sakes, *a pencil!* (KAREN *is frantically looking through her purse.* SAM, *into the phone*) . . . One seventy-five escalating up to three and a quarter . . . (KAREN *takes a lipstick out of her purse and hobbles quickly to* SAM. *She hands it to him*) Hold it. (*He writes on the pad*) One seventy-five up to three and a quarter . . . (*He stops writing and looks at* KAREN) That's a lipstick.

KAREN (*Taking the empty Bendel box from the chair*) I don't have a pencil.

SAM   Then why do you give me a lipstick?

KAREN Because I don't have a pencil. It's shocking pink but it writes.

(*Puts the box into the wastebasket next to the dresser*)

SAM (*He glares at her. Into the phone*) All right, I'm going to go over my figures here. If Henderson calls or the contracts come in, bring them right over. What's that? (*He laughs*) Yes! Well, it's like we were saying the other night, it's the old badger game. (*He laughs again.* KAREN *mocks his private joke with* MISS MC-CORMAC *as she hobbles back into the bedroom*) . . . All right, I'll speak to you later. And thank you, Miss McCormack. (*He hangs up*) A hundred and seventy-five thousand dollar contract, you give me a lipstick.

(*Puts the lipstick down on the table next to the chair*)

KAREN (*Hobbles out of the bathroom with the vase*) I'd have given you blood but it isn't blue.

SAM All right, don't test me, because I've got enough of a headache. (*He rubs his eyes with his thumb and index finger, opens the case and takes out a bottle of aspirin. She limps into the living room and places the vase on the desk. He looks at her*) And for God's sakes, Karen, stop hobbling around. I don't feel like listening to thump, thump, thump!

KAREN (*She sighs*) And happy anniversary to you.

SAM What?

KAREN Forget it.

(*Sits at the desk and takes off her other galosh and shoe*)

SAM (*Moving to the bathroom with the aspirin*) What are you talking about? . . . It's not our anniversary.

KAREN Today is December fourteenth, isn't it?

SAM Yes.

KAREN So. We're married twenty-four years today.

SAM (*Looks at her incredulously*) Are you serious?

KAREN We're not married twenty-four years today?

SAM No.
(*Comes out of the bathroom with a glass of water and takes an aspirin*)

KAREN We're not married twenty-four years?

SAM No.

KAREN . . . We're not married?

SAM Tomorrow is our anniversary and we're married twenty-three years.
(*Puts the glass down on the dresser and moves into the living room*)

KAREN (*Looks at him*) . . . Are you sure?

SAM What do you mean, am I sure? I know when our anniversary is. December fifteenth, we're married twenty-three years. How can you make a mistake like that?

KAREN All right, don't get so excited, and it's not such a big mistake because I didn't get you a present . . . You're sure it's not the fourteenth?

SAM I go through this with you every year. When it comes to money or dates or ages, you are absolutely unbelievable. (*Turns, exasperated, and goes to the bedroom*) We were married December fifteenth, nineteen forty-five . . .

KAREN   Then I'm right. Twenty-*four* years.

SAM   Forty-five from sixty-eight is *twenty-three!*

KAREN   Then I'm wrong. (*Shrugs*) Math isn't one of my best subjects.

SAM   (*Hanging his jacket over the dresser chair*) This isn't math, this is people's *lives!* (*Moves back to* KAREN) How old are you?

KAREN   What?

SAM   It's a simple question. How old are you?

KAREN   (*She's reluctant to answer and moves to the window*) I don't want to play.

SAM   I can't believe it. You really don't know how old you are.

KAREN   I know how old I am. But you get me nervous. Promise you won't leave me if I'm wrong . . . I'll be forty-nine in April. (SAM *stares at her in the disbelief, crosses back into the bedroom and wearily leans against the closet door.* KAREN *follows him*) . . . Isn't that right?

SAM   No, but you're close.

KAREN   I'm not going to be forty-nine?

SAM   Not *this* April. *This* April you're going to be forty-eight. How the hell can you make a mistake like that? Can't you add?
        (*Taking several contracts out of the attaché case*)

KAREN   All right, don't talk to me like I'm a child. I'm a forty-eight-year-old woman.

SAM   But the thing that infuriates me is that you make the mistake the wrong way. Why don't you make yourself younger instead of older, the way other women do?

KAREN   Okay, I'm forty-seven. (*Throws herself on the bed and poses sexily*) So how do I look to you now?

SAM   I've got work to do. I've got a very important meeting at eight o'clock in the morning.
(*Crosses to the desk and sits*)

KAREN   (*Sitting up in bed*)   Oh, come on, Sam, where's your sense of humor? I think it's cute as hell that I don't know how old I am.

SAM   (*Starts to look over the papers*)   I can't even think straight. I've had five meetings this morning, four teeth capped, and I haven't even had my Metrecal. (*He crosses to the phone in the living room*) I'd better eat something.
(*Picks up the phone*)

KAREN   I just ordered hors d'oeuvres.

SAM   Not for me. You know I'm on nine hundred calories a day. (*Into the phone*) Room service, please. (*He turns and looks in the mirror*) . . . My God, who the hell is that? Will you look at my eyes? I have no pupils left. (*He turns to* KAREN) Come here. Look at this. Do you see any pupils?

KAREN   (*Crosses and looks into the mirror*)   Yes, Sam. I see two gorgeous pupils . . .

SAM   (*Still looking in the mirror*)   Where? Where? I

don't have a pupil in my head. Would you get my
eye drops out of the case . . .

KAREN (*Crossing to the case on the bed*)   I think you've
been overworking, Sam. I haven't seen you two nights
this month.

SAM (*Stretches his arms*)   I really could use some sun.
And about a month of sleep.

KAREN (*Searching through the case*)   Hey, why don't
we go down to Jamaica for a couple weeks? Just the
two of us. We haven't done that in years.

SAM (*Into the phone, pacing*)   Oh, hello, room service,
where were you? . . . Listen, I'd like a plate of cold
roast beef, medium rare, very lean. You know what
very lean is? . . . No, it doesn't mean no fat . . . It
means *absolutely* no fat . . . and I want a salad, *no
dressing,* a half grapefruit and a pot of black coffee . . .
And I'd appreciate it as soon as possible . . . Wait a
second. (*To* KAREN, *who has entered the living room
with eye drops*) Where are we again?

KAREN   719, Plaza Hotel, New York, twenty-three, New
York.

SAM (*Into the phone*)   719 . . . As soon as you can. (*He
hangs up, moves down to* KAREN *at the couch*) What's
wrong with you today?

KAREN   You wouldn't believe it, but fifteen minutes ago
I was the happiest woman on earth . . . Sit down, I'll
put your pupils back in.

SAM (*Hand extended*)   I can do it myself.

KAREN   I know you can, Sam, but I like to put your
eye drops in. (*He lies down on the sofa with his head*

16

on the arm and she moves to look down at him from the side of the sofa) It's the only time lately you look at me.
(She poises the eye dropper)

SAM *(Looks up at her)* . . . I'm sorry.

KAREN You are?

SAM I haven't been nice to *anyone* the past couple of weeks.

KAREN You sounded swell to Miss McCormack.

SAM Put the eye drops in.

KAREN *(Bending down over the arm of the sofa)* First give an old lady a kiss.
(He gives her a soft, gentle kiss)

SAM I give you my permission to hate me.

KAREN *(Straightens up)* I'll save it for later. Open your gorgeous pupils.
(KAREN fills the dropper with fluid)

SAM Eight months I've been working on this deal and suddenly today my two top men in the office come down with the flu and I've got to do everything myself. *(She puts the drops in his eye. He jumps up)* Aaghh!
(He grabs his eye in pain)

KAREN What's the matter?

SAM *(Sitting up)* You *drop* them in, you don't *push* them in.

KAREN I'm sorry, you moved your head.

SAM I moved my head because you were stabbing my

eyeball. (*Gets up and peers in the mirror over the fireplace*) Oh, damn it!

KAREN   All right, don't panic, Sam, I'm sorry.

SAM   Why do you think they call it a dropper? If they wanted you to stab people, they would call it a stabber. (*Grabs it from her*) Give it to me, I'll do it myself.
(*Lies back down on the sofa and begins to put drops in both eyes*)

KAREN   You mean that's the end of being nice to each other?

SAM   I don't know what we're doing in a hotel anyway.

KAREN   What's the Plaza got to do with my stabbing your eyeball?

SAM   Because it's insane being here, that's why. I've got work to do tonight, I don't know how I'm going to concentrate.

KAREN   You've got to sleep *some*place tonight. The painter says it's going to take two days for the house to dry.

SAM   Yes, but why *now*? Do it in the spring. This is my busy time of the year.
(SAM *puts the eye drops on the coffee table and crosses to the bedroom*)

KAREN   I know, but it's not the painter's busy time of the year. In the spring he doesn't want to know you.

SAM   Why didn't you ask me first?
(KAREN *follows him into the bedroom*)

KAREN   I never see you . . . I saw the painter.

Photo Credit: *Martha Swope*

Maureen Stapleton as Karen Nash
George C. Scott as Sam Nash
"Visitor From Mamaroneck"

SAM   You could have checked with my secretary. (*He goes into the bathroom*)

KAREN   I did. She said go ahead and paint the house. (*She takes his coat from the bed and hangs it in the closet*)

SAM'S VOICE   Of all times of the year. Did you bring my things? Toothbrush? Pajamas?

KAREN   I brought your toothbrush.

SAM'S VOICE   You forgot my pajamas?

KAREN   (*Plops down on the bed*)   I didn't forget them, I just didn't bring them.
(SAM *comes out of the bathroom wiping his eyes on the towel*)

SAM   Why not?

KAREN   Because this is Suite 719 at the Plaza and I just didn't think you'd want your pajamas tonight.

SAM   You know I can't sleep without pajamas. (*He returns to the bathroom*)

KAREN   (*Yelling after him*)   I took that into consideration . . .

SAM   What?

KAREN   Never mind. They've got shops in the lobby. (*Gets up and picks up the phone next to the bed*) Should I send for their catalog or will you take pot luck?

SAM   Heh. You know what a pair of pajamas would cost at the Plaza? Forty, fifty dollars.

KAREN   You want me to send a bellhop to Bloomingdale's? (*Hangs up the phone*)

SAM (*Comes out of the bathroom*) I don't understand you. One lousy little bag is all you had to pack.

KAREN Forgive me. It's my busy time of the year.

SAM Karen, do me a favor. Don't get brittle. (*Crosses to the desk in the living room*) I'm very shaky right now and one good crack and I go right to the dry cleaner's . . . Boy, could I use a nice, big, cold double martini.

(*He sits and begins to examine the contracts*)

KAREN (*Follows him into the living and leans on the chest of drawers*) Don't get angry, but can I make a suggestion? Why don't you have a nice, big, cold double martini?

SAM Are you serious? You know how many calories are in a double martini?

KAREN (*Shrugs*) Four or five million?

SAM You know my metabolism. One double martini, and right in front of your eyes I get flabby.

KAREN You used to get sexy.
(*She takes a sheet from a pile of stationery in the chest*)

SAM (*Gets up with the papers to sit in more comfort on the sofa*) Well, now I get flabby. Unless I watch myself like a hawk . . . (*As he passes the fireplace mirror, he pauses, admiring his waistline*) which I think I manage to do.
(*Sits on the sofa*)

KAREN (*She starts to fold the piece of stationery*) I like you flabby.

SAM What does that mean?

KAREN (*Still folding the paper*) It means I like you flabby. I admit you look like one of the Pepsi generation, but it seems a little unnatural to me. A man of your age ought to have a couple of pounds of skin hanging over his belt.

SAM Well, I'm sorry to disappoint you.

KAREN I'm not disappointed, I'm uncomfortable. I watch you when you get undressed at night. Nothing moves. You're vacuum packed. When you open your belt I expect it to go like a can of coffee—*Pzzzzzz!*
(*She continues folding*)

SAM Do you think it's easy with my metabolism to keep my weight down? Do you know what it's like to have a business luncheon at the Villa Capri and watch someone slop down a bowl of spaghetti and I'm munching on a hearts of lettuce salad?

KAREN My compliments to your restraint.

SAM I go through torture to maintain my weight.

KAREN I have nothing but admiration for your waistline.
(*She is through folding*)

SAM But you like me flabby.

KAREN We all have our little perversions.

SAM Can we drop the subject?

KAREN Like a baked potato.

SAM Thank you.

KAREN You're welcome.
(*She aims her finished paper airplane across the room and lets it fly*)

SAM (*Gets up and paces angrily*) . . . Why do you like me flabby?

KAREN Is the floor open again?

SAM No. Forget it.

KAREN It's forgotten.

SAM What was I just doing?

KAREN Watching yourself like a hawk.
(*She crosses to the bedroom and begins to fold her negligée at the dresser.* SAM *returns to the sofa. There is a silence. Finally*)

SAM Look, I just want to say one more thing and then the discussion is closed. (KAREN *puts down the negligée and crosses back to the sofa in the living room*) I'm at the athletic club three, four times a week watching men at least ten years younger than me huffing and puffing trying to sweat off a couple of ounces that goes right back on after the cocktail hour. Now maybe you don't consider it a monumental achievement, but my weight hasn't changed in six years. I'm still one seventy-seven on the scale.

KAREN So am I. (*Crosses to the bedroom and puts the negligée away in the chest*) Now you know why I like you flabby . . . The subject is closed.
(*She crosses to the chair and sits.* SAM, *upset, remains in the living room. They contemplate the floor a few seconds*)

SAM . . . Hey, Karen.

KAREN Yah, Sam . . .

SAM Let's not fight.

KAREN   It's all right with me, Sam.

SAM   . . . Let's be nice to each other.

KAREN   Okay . . . Who goes first?
(SAM *gets up and starts for the bedroom. He stops
at the door . . . trying to find words*)

SAM   Karen . . .

KAREN   (*Looks up*)   Yes, Sam?

SAM   (*This doesn't seem to be the time to bring up whatever is on his mind*)   Nothing . . . I'm going to do a
little work, okay?
(*He goes back into the living room and sits on
the sofa*)

KAREN   (*Still sitting. Without malice*)   You don't even
remember this room, you louse.

SAM   What's that?

KAREN   (*Gets up and crosses into the living room*)   I
may not know how old I am, but I sure as hell remember we spent our honeymoon night in Suite 719
at the Plaza Hotel and this is definitely 719 because
I just tipped the bellhop an entire dollar.

SAM   (*Looks at the room for the first time*)   Was this
the room?

KAREN   Oh, Christ.
(*She sits on the arm of the sofa*)

SAM   (*Gets up and looks about*)   Wait a minute, I think
you're right. (*He looks into the bedroom*) Sure, this
looks like the suite. Only it was decorated differently.
This room was blue.

KAREN (*Going into the bedroom*) That was you. You were in the Navy. The bedroom was green.

SAM   I think you're mistaken. The bedroom was blue.

KAREN   You're probably confusing it with some other honeymoon . . . (*Sitting on the bed*) Hey, Sam, remember we had dinner here in the bedroom?

SAM.   No.

KAREN   Yes. We had dinner here in the bedroom. Do you remember what we had?

SAM   For dinner? Twenty-three years ago?

KAREN   *I* remember. You remember too. Take a guess.

SAM   Karen, I don't remember.

KAREN   Yes, you do. Think about it a second.

SAM   I thought about it. I don't remember.

KAREN   We had a bottle of champagne and a tray full of hors d'oeuvres. And we left all the anchovies in the drawer.
(*Indicates the night table*)

SAM   Oh.
(*Crosses and looks out the living room window*)

KAREN   See. It's coming back to you. (*Notices him looking out the window*) If you're looking for the Savoy-Plaza, it's not there.
(*She goes to the bedroom window and follows his gaze*)

SAM (*Looking out the window*) I'm looking at the Pierre.

KAREN There it is.

SAM . . . Karen.

KAREN What?

SAM (*Still looking out the window*) It was 819. (KAREN
Steps back from the window and looks at SAM. SAM
turns and looks at her) We were in 819, not 719.

KAREN (*She glares at him and grits her teeth with hos-
tility*) You're wrong!

SAM I'm not wrong, I'm right. We were in 819. I'm
right.

KAREN (*Angry*) Don't keep saying you're right like
you're right. You're wrong. We were in 719.

SAM I'll prove it to you. Come here. (KAREN *joins him
at the living-room window*) Remember, I had my
binoculars, we were watching that couple getting undressed in the Pierre? They were on the eighth floor.
I remember because we were looking for them the next
night. We called them "The Couple on the Eighth
Floor."

KAREN I don't know what you called them, I called
them "The Couple on the Seventh Floor."
    (*She walks away angrily into the bedroom*)

SAM Look, it's pointless to argue about it. It's not
important.

KAREN (*From the bedroom*) If it's pointless, then why
are you pointing it out?

SAM Because you made an issue of it.

KAREN (*Crossing to the bedroom door*) Maybe I made

25

an issue of saying we were in 719, but *you* made an issue of proving to me we *weren't* in 719.

SAM All right, Karen.
(*He walks away to the fireplace*)

KAREN Don't tell me, "All right, Karen." If I thought it was 719, why didn't you have the decency to let me just go on in my ignorance and think it was 719?

SAM Okay. Okay. I'm sorry. It was 719.

KAREN Aw, forget it. It was 819.
(*Moves back into the bedroom*)

SAM (*Rushing into the bedroom*) No, no. As a matter of fact, you're right. I just remembered. It really was 719.

KAREN I don't want it 719. I want it 819 . . . Look, why don't you go inside and lose some weight? (*That was a nasty remark.* SAM *glares at* KAREN, *then goes into the living room, reassures himself with a glance at his waistline in the fireplace mirror, picks up his work papers and sits.* KAREN *realizes what she's done. She crosses to the living room and embraces him*) I'm sorry, Sam. (SAM *nods his head and looks at his papers.* KAREN *moves around the sofa*) . . . We're some lousy couple, aren't we? . . . Aren't we?

SAM. (*Doesn't look up*) Mmm.

KAREN Mmm what?
(*Sitting on the arm of the sofa*)

SAM (*Looks up*) Mmm, yes, we're some lousy couple.

KAREN (*Without malice*) That's what I said. First thing we agreed on today.

SAM   Look, Karen, I really don't mean to be rude, but I *must* work on these estimates tonight. You understand.

KAREN   Sure, I understand.

SAM   I explained to you that Sid and Walter suddenly came down with the flu—

KAREN   It's all right, Sam. You're excused . . . (*She wanders aimlessly about the room. Catching sight of herself in the mirror over the chest, she examines her figure and then decides to do some exercises, which she quickly gives up. She sits on the arm of the sofa next to* SAM) Do you have any good estimates for me to read?

SAM   Isn't there anything to read in the bedroom?

KAREN   (*Shrugs*) "Check-out time is three o'clock." That's all I could find . . . Don't worry about me. I'll find something to do.
      (SAM *goes back to his papers.* KAREN *puts her arms around his shoulders and rocks him playfully from side to side, much to* SAM's *displeasure. Suddenly she releases him, goes to the front door, opens it and goes into the hall*)

SAM   What are you doing?

KAREN   (*Coming back into the room*) Looking for the waiter.

SAM   Call him up.

KAREN   I thought I'd look in the hall first. Gives me something to do. (*She goes back out into the hall*) Nope, don't see him. (*Comes back in and closes the door*) In five minutes I'll call. See? I'll alternate them.

SAM Karen, please.

KAREN (*Crosses to him and takes his arm*) Oh, come on. Forget your crummy old papers and take me to a dirty movie. (*Tries to pull him out of the sofa*) Come on, Sam. Let's go.

SAM Stop it, Karen.

KAREN You know what's playing on Sixth Avenue? *Cat House Confidential* and *Ursula the Slut*. I passed it in the cab, I swear on my mother's life.

SAM Don't be ridiculous.

KAREN (*Kneeling by the sofa*) Are you afraid we'll be recognized? We'll buy beards in the five-and-ten.

SAM If you want to go, go yourself.

KAREN What happens if I get picked up?

SAM Call me and I won't wait up for you.

KAREN (*Hugging him*) Oh, good, you've got your sense of humor back. All right, just take a walk with me. A ten-minute walk and I'll leave you alone.

SAM Maybe later. We'll see.

KAREN (*Getting up and pacing*) No movies . . . no walk. (*She sits on top of the chest of drawers and picks up* What to Do in New York *magazine and skims through it. There is a silence. Finally*) Feel like going back to the house and watching the paint dry? (SAM, *at the end of his patience, gets up with the papers and moves into the bedroom*) . . . I'm just trying to think of something we can do together.
    (*The doorbell rings*)

SAM (*Pacing in the bedroom*) Shall I get it, or is that something you'd like for us to do together?

KAREN Listen, I'll even take nastiness. It's not much, but it's a start.
> (KAREN *crosses to the door and opens it. It's the* WAITER *with the food on a roller table. He is a middle-aged Puerto Rican*)

WAITER Good evening.

KAREN (*Smiles*) Hello.
> (*The* WAITER *rolls the table in*)

WAITER Would you like the table near the window?

KAREN (*Moves toward the bedroom*) Sam, would you like the table near the window?

SAM (*Disinterested*) It doesn't make any difference.

KAREN (*Sweetly, to the* WAITER) It doesn't make any difference.

WAITER (*Leaving the table up near the window*) Shall I leave it here?

KAREN Sam, should he leave it there?

SAM (*Throwing the contract on the bed and moving to the doorway*) Here, there, anywhere, it doesn't make any difference.

KAREN (*Shrugs, smiles at the* WAITER) Here, there, anywhere. It doesn't make any difference.

WAITER (*Takes a chair from the desk and puts it to the right of the table*) Yes, Ma'am.
> (*He gets the armchair from the right of the sofa and brings it to the table*)

SAM (*To the* WAITER) You don't have to set up the chairs.

KAREN (*To the* WAITER) You don't have to set up the chairs.

WAITER Yes, Ma'am.
  (*He starts to put the armchair back*)

SAM All right, leave them, you've done it already.

KAREN Yes, why don't you just leave the chairs. They're all set up.
  (*The* WAITER *puts the chair back at the table*)

SAM Can I have the bill, please?

WAITER Yes, sir.
  (*Takes the bill and a pencil to* SAM. KAREN *looks at the tray of hors d'oeuvres on the table*)

KAREN (*Sweetly*) Oh, look at all the anchovies.

SAM (*Signing the bill*) Didn't you tell them you didn't want anchovies?

WAITER (*To* KAREN) You didn't want anchovies?

KAREN (*Doesn't want more trouble*) No, no. I asked for anchovies. I'm a very big fan of anchovies.

SAM (*Hands the bill to the* WAITER) That'll be all, thank you.

KAREN Yes, that'll be all, thank you.

WAITER And thank you.
  (*Crosses to the door*)

KAREN (*Looks at the table*) Wait a minute. The champagne. Where's the champagne?

WAITER   No champagne? (*Looks at the check*) You're right. They forgot the champagne.

KAREN   But the anchovies they remembered.

SAM   (*Returning to the bedroom*) I can't drink anything now, I've got work to do. What do you need a whole bottle of champagne for?

KAREN   It's our anniversary. (*To the* WAITER) It's our anniversary.

WAITER   Oh, congratulations.

KAREN   (*Sitting on the arm of the chair at the table*) Thank you. We're married twenty-three or twenty-four years today or tomorrow.

WAITER   Then you want the champagne?

KAREN   With two grown children in college.

WAITER   Oh? That's wonderful.

KAREN   (*Shrugs*) You think so? He's flunking out and she's majoring in dirty clothes.

SAM   (*Greatly irritated, moves back to the living room*) He's not flunking out. Why do you say he's flunking out? (*Controls himself. To the* WAITER) That'll be all, thank you.

WAITER   If you don't want the champagne, I'll cross it out of the bill.

SAM   She doesn't want the champagne. Cross it off the bill.
       (*Crosses back to the bedroom*)

KAREN   (*To the* WAITER) I *want* the champagne. Don't cross it off the bill. Bring me a bottle and *one* glass.

WAITER   Yes, Ma'am.

SAM (*From the bedroom*)   That'll be all, thank you.

KAREN   Yes, that'll be all, thank you.

WAITER (*Opening the door*)   When you want me to take the table, just ring.

KAREN (*Moving to the* WAITER)   Yes, I'll ring when I want you to take the table.

WAITER   Thank you . . . And again, congratulations.
   (*He exits.* SAM *crosses to the table and takes the cover off a dish*)

KAREN   (*At the mantel*)   . . . Did you hear that, Sam? We're being congratulated on being married to each other.

SAM (*Disgusted, slams the cover back on the dish*)   I asked for lean roast beef. That is not lean roast beef. (*Moves to the sofa and sits, taking a contract from the coffee table*)

KAREN (*Contemplatively*)   You know how many people we know who are still married as long as us? One other couple. The Shelley's . . . The most boring people I ever met.

SAM (*Cannot contain himself any more*)   Why do you talk to the waiter like that?

KAREN   Like what?
   (*Sits at the table and begins to serve herself*)

SAM   Like you've known him for twenty years. You just met him. He walked in here two minutes ago with fatty roast beef. It's none of his business how our son is doing in school.

KAREN   I was just having a conversation. I get lonely, I like to talk to people.

SAM   He's a waiter. Talk to him about food.

KAREN   I did something wrong again. I'm sorry, Sam. When he brings the champagne I'll hide behind the drapes.

SAM   You don't have to hide. Just don't tell him our personal problems, that's all.

KAREN   What should I do, lie?

SAM   Certainly, lie. Everybody else does. Tell them you have a beautiful and devoted daughter. Tell them you have a brilliant son who's on the dean's list. Tell them you're only forty-two years old.

KAREN   There's no point to it. In two years I'll be fifty. Who's going to like me better if I'm only forty-two?

SAM   You don't have to revel in it like it's some kind of an accomplishment.

KAREN   I'm not insane about getting older. It happens to everyone. It's happened to you. You're fifty-one years old.

SAM   (*Nods his head in exasperation*) That's the difference between us. I don't accept it. I don't have to accept being fifty-one. (*Getting up and moving to her*) I don't accept getting older.

KAREN   Good luck to you. You'll be the youngest one in the cemetery.

SAM   We can't even have a normal discussion any more. (*He stalks into the bedroom, closes the door and stretches out on the bed*)

KAREN Accept being fifty-one and I'll have a normal discussion. (*Stops as* SAM *closes the door*) . . . Aren't you going to have your dinner? (*Gets up and examines the plate of meat. Holds up a piece to the bedroom door and calls to* SAM) Sam, I found some very lean roast beef. (*She nibbles on a piece*) Come inside and see how thin I'm getting. (*The doorbell rings*) . . . Hey, come on. The champagne is here. (*She opens the door to the bedroom and calls in*) If you don't come out, I'll tell the waiter you wear dentures. (*She crosses and opens the front door.* JEAN MCCORMACK *stands there. She is* SAM'S *secretary. She is a trim, attractive woman about twenty-eight. She is neatly dressed, bright, cheerful and smilingly efficient*) . . . Oh! Hello, Miss McCormack.

JEAN Hello, Mrs. Nash. I hope I'm not disturbing you.

KAREN No, no, not at all. Mr. Nash and I were just sitting around, joking. Come in.
(*Still holding the roast beef in her hand*)

JEAN Thank you. (*She enters the room, closing the door behind her*) I hate to barge in this way, but I have some papers that need Mr. Nash's signature immediately.

KAREN Certainly. (*Calls out*) Sam. It's Miss McCormack. (*To* JEAN) It is *Miss* McCormack now, isn't it?

JEAN (*Taking several contracts out of her brief case*) It *was* Mrs. Colby last year. This year it's Miss McCormack again.

KAREN (*Sitting on the arm of the sofa*) Oh. You're lucky you can remember. I've been married so long,

if I got divorced, I'd have to make up a maiden name
. . . Have you had your dinner yet?
(Indicates the roast beef in her hand)

JEAN *(Laying out some contracts on the coffee table in front of the sofa)* I don't have dinner, thank you.

KAREN No dinner? Ever?

JEAN *(Getting her glasses and a pen from her purse on the console table behind the sofa)* I have a large breakfast, a moderate lunch and a snack before going to bed. On this job I've worked late so often, I had to readjust my eating routine. Now I'm used to it.
(SAM gets up from the bed and moves into the living room)

KAREN Oh. Well, I can understand that. I miss a lot of dinners with Mr. Nash too.

SAM Oh, hello. You got them, huh?
(Sits on the sofa and examines a contract)

JEAN Just came in. All ready for signature.

KAREN *(To JEAN)* How about some black coffee? Or would that fill you up?

JEAN Black coffee would be fine, thank you.

KAREN One black coffee coming up. Sam, would you like some black coffee?

SAM No.

KAREN That's no black coffee and one black coffee.
(KAREN crosses to the table; SAM is looking over the contracts. JEAN sits next to him. KAREN pours coffee)

SAM Why is there an adjustment on this figure?

JEAN (*Looks at it*) There was a clerical omission on the Cincinnati tabulations. It didn't show up on the 1400 but I rechecked it with my own files and made the correction. (*Points to respective pages of the contract*) So that item 17B should read three hundred and twenty-five thousand and disregard the figure on 17A.

KAREN Cream and sugar?

JEAN No, thank you.

SAM But this should have been caught on the IBM.

JEAN It should have, but it wasn't. Obviously it wasn't fed properly.

KAREN No cream and no sugar or no cream and yes, sugar?

JEAN No cream and *no* sugar.

KAREN So it's yes, no cream and no sugar.

SAM Did you call this to Purcell's attention?

KAREN (*Handing a cup to* JEAN) Would you like some pastry or cookies? I could call down. They have beautiful pastry and cookies here.

JEAN This is fine thank you. (*To* SAM) Mr. Purcell says this happened once before this month. He can't pin it down until he rechecks the whole 66 file.

KAREN (*Leaning on the console table behind the sofa*) You're sure? A sandwich? A Welsh rarebit?

JEAN No, I'm really quite happy, thank you. (*Takes saccharine from her purse and puts it in the coffee*)

SAM Well, I'm just going to have to go over this whole thing tonight with Howard. If we give Henderson any room for doubt, we can blow our entire presentation.

JEAN (*Sips the coffee*) I told him there was a possibility of this, so he made plans to stay in town tonight.

SAM Damn! Of all nights to have this happen. (*Putting down the contract*) What time is it now?

JEAN (*Looks at her watch*) Ten past five.

KAREN (*Looking over* JEAN'*s shoulder*) Ten past five.

SAM All right, you tell Howard I'll meet him in the office between six fifteen and six thirty. Tell him I want to see every one of last year's 1400 forms.

KAREN (*Moving around the sofa to* SAM) You're going to the office? Tonight?

SAM It can't be helped, Karen. (JEAN *puts her coffee cup down*) We're having that same damned trouble with the computer again.

KAREN I could go with you. Maybe all it needs is a little dusting.

SAM Something in that office sure as hell needs dusting. (*Getting up and moving to the bedroom.* JEAN *gathers up the contracts and moves to put them in the brief case at the console table*) All right, Miss McCormack, why don't you hop in a cab now and get started on these figures with Howard? I just want to clean up and I'll meet you in about twenty minutes.

JEAN Yes, sir.

SAM I hope I'm not ruining any plans you had for tonight.

JEAN   When I saw the figures this morning, I expected it. (*Closes the case.* SAM *takes a bottle of pills from his attaché case and crosses to the bathroom*) Mrs. Nash, thank you very much for the coffee.

KAREN   You really should eat something. You'll faint right over the IBM machine.

JEAN   (*Opening the front door*)   I'll be all right.

KAREN   (*Moving to her above the sofa*)   It's a pity you can't stay two more minutes. I just ordered champagne. Can I tell her why, Sam?

SAM   (*Returns from the bathroom, having taken pills. Throws the pills back into his case*)   What's that?
(*Drinks from a glass on the dresser. Takes his jacket from the back of the chair and puts in on*)

KAREN   Well, I'm not supposed to go around blurting these things out, but it's our twenty-third anniversary . . .

JEAN   Oh? I didn't know. Congratulations.

KAREN   (*To* JEAN, *but for* SAM's *benefit*)   Thank you . . . Yes, life has been very good to me. I have a beautiful and devoted daughter, a brilliant son who's on the dean's list, I'm forty-two years old, what more can I ask?

SAM   (*Moving into the living room*)   Karen, Miss McCormack has to get back to the office.
(SAM *goes back into the bedroom, takes hairbrushes from an overnight bag and brushes his hair in front of the closet mirror*)

KAREN   Oh, I'm sorry. (*To* JEAN) Don't let him work you too late.

JEAN   It's all right. I'm used to it now. Best wishes again, Mrs. Nash.

KAREN   (*As* JEAN *starts out*)   Thanks, dear. And see that he buys me a nice gift.

JEAN (*Smiles*)   I definitely will.
  (*Closes the door*)

KAREN   (*To* SAM)   What a sweet girl. That's a very sweet girl, Sam.

SAM   Karen, listen, I'm very sorry about tonight. It just can't be helped.
  (*Puts the brushes back*)

KAREN   That's a sweet, young, skinny girl.

SAM   (*Takes a cordless electric razor from his attaché case and crosses to the bathroom*)   The thing is, if I leave now maybe I can still get back in time for us to have a late dinner.

KAREN   (*Enters the bedroom and sits in the armchair*)   Oh, don't worry about me, Sam. (SAM *begins to shave*) I understand. I just feel badly for you. You could have really relaxed tonight, and instead you'll be cooped up in that stuffy office until all hours working over some boring contracts with your smooth-shaven face.

SAM   (*Still shaving, moves into the bedroom*)   Well, I can't very well walk through the lobby of the Plaza Hotel with a stubbly chin.
  (*Returns to the bathroom*)

KAREN   They wouldn't let you into the elevator. Don't forget your Jade East.

SAM'S VOICE   My what?

39

KAREN   Your sexy cologne. The doorman will never get you a cab if you don't smell nice.

SAM (*Enters the bedroom. Looks at* KAREN *for a moment and then shuts the razor off*) What are you doing, Karen?

KAREN   Oh, I'm just joking. Can't you tell when I'm kidding around any more, Sam?

SAM   No, I can't.
   (*Crosses around the bed and puts the razor back in the case*)

KAREN (*Playfully pats his fanny, and then sits on the bed*) Well, of course I am. I'm just teasing you by intimating you're having an affair with your secretary.

SAM   I see.
   (*Takes his overcoat from the top of the bureau and puts it on*)

KAREN   Are you, Sam? Is sweet, skinny Miss McCormack your mistress?

SAM   For God's sakes, Karen, what kind of a thing is that to say?

KAREN   If you're not, it's a lousy thing to say. If you are, it's a hell of a question.

SAM   I'm not even going to dignify that with an answer.

KAREN (*On her knees, bouncing up and down like a child*) Oh, come on, Sam, dignify it. I'm dying to know. Just tell me if you're having an affair with her or not.

SAM   And you'll believe me?

KAREN   Of course.

SAM   No, I'm not having an affair with her.

KAREN (*Giving a big smile*)   Yes, you are.

SAM   Curses, trapped again. (*Looks out the window*)
It looks like snow. I hope I can get a cab.

KAREN (*Starting to take off her hairpiece*)   Even if you're
not, Sam, it's all right if you do. I approve of Miss
McCormack. She's a nice girl.

SAM (*Getting his attaché case from the bed*)   Thank
you. She'll be pleased to know. Look, I could call
downstairs and get you a ticket for a show tonight.
There's no reason for you to sit alone like this. Is
there something you'd like to see?

KAREN (*Smiles*)   Yeah. What you and Miss McCormack
will be doing later.

SAM   Really, Karen, I find this in very poor taste.
(*Moving to the living room, puts the attaché case
down on the console table behind the sofa*)

KAREN (*Getting a brush from the overnight case*)   Why?
I'm just being honest again. I'm saying that if at this
stage of your life you wanted to have a small, quiet
affair with a young, skinny woman, I would understand.
(*Sits back on the bed and begins to brush out her
hairpiece*)

SAM (*Stops abruptly in his gathering of the contracts
from the coffee table and returns to the bedroom*)
What do you mean, at this stage of my life?

KAREN (*Continues her brushing*)   Well, you're blankety

years old. I would say the number but I know you don't accept it. And I realize that when a man becomes blankety-one or blankety-two, he is feeling insecure, that he's losing his virility (*Smiles broadly at* SAM), and that a quiet fling may be the best thing for him. I know, I read the New York *Post*.

SAM   I'm glad to know I have Rose Franzblau's permission.

KAREN   And mine if you really want it.

SAM (*Yells*)   Well, I don't want it and *I'm not having an affair!*

KAREN   Then why are you yelling?

SAM (*Crosses to the living room*)   Because this is an idiotic conversation.

KAREN (*Collapses on the bed*)   Oh, Sam, I'm so glad.

SAM (*Takes the contracts from the coffee table and puts them in his case*)   Now you're happy? You're happy because *now* you don't think I'm having an affair?

KAREN   Well, of course I'm happy. You think I'm some kind of a domestic mental case? I don't want you having an affair. I'm just saying that if you *are* having one, I understand.

SAM (*Crosses to the bedroom and picks up a contract from the bed*)   Karen, I have a hard night's work ahead of me. I'll be back about twelve.
      (*Starts to leave*)

KAREN   Sam, stay and talk to me for five minutes.

SAM   They're waiting for me at the office. I've got work to do.

KAREN You've got help in the office. I've been with
the firm longer than all of them . . . (*After a moment,*
SAM *sits on the edge of the bureau*) Sam, I know we
haven't been very happy lately. I know you've been
busy, you may not have noticed it, but we have definitely not been very happy.

SAM Yes, Karen, I've noticed it.

KAREN (*Continues to brush her hairpiece*) What's
wrong? We have a twelve-room house in the country,
two sweet children, a maid who doesn't drink. Is there
something we're missing?

SAM I—don't know.

KAREN Can you at least think about it? I need hints,
Sam . . . (*Quoting*) "Is there something else you
want?" (SAM *doesn't answer*) "Is there something I
can give you that I'm not giving you?" (*Again no
answer*) . . . Could you please speak up, we're closing
in ten minutes.

SAM It's me, Karen, it not you.
(*Crosses to the living room, puts the contract in
his case, closes it*)

KAREN (*Puts her hair and brush on the dresser and follows him into the living room*) I'll buy that. What's
wrong with you, Sam?

SAM (*There is a long pause*) I don't know . . . (*Moves
to the mantel and then paces in front of the sofa*) I
don't know if you can understand this . . . but when I
came home after the war . . . I had my whole life in
front of me. And all I dreamed about, all I wanted, was
to get married, and to have children . . . and to make

a success of my life . . . Well, I was very lucky . . . I I got it all . . . Marriage, the children . . . more money than I ever dreamed of making . . .

KAREN (*Sitting on the sofa*) Then what is it you want?

SAM (*Stopping by the fireplace*) I just want to do it all over again . . . I would like to start the whole damned thing right from the beginning.

KAREN (*Long pause*) I see. Well, frankly, Sam, I don't think the Navy will take you again.

SAM (*Smiles ruefully*) Well, it won't be because I can't pass the physical. (*Takes his case and starts for the door again*) I told you it's stupid talking about it. It'll work itself out. If not, I'll dye my hair.
(*He opens the door*)

KAREN You know what I think? I think you want to get out and you don't know how to tell me.

SAM (*Stops in the door. Turns back to* KAREN) That's not true.

KAREN Which isn't? That you want to get out or that you don't know how to tell me?

SAM Why do you always start the most serious discussions in our life when I'm halfway out the door?

KAREN If that's what you want, just tell me straight out. Just say, "Karen, there's no point in going on." I'd rather hear it from you personally, than getting a message on our service.

SAM Look, we'll talk about it when I get back, okay?
(*He starts out again*)

KAREN (*Can no longer contain herself. There is none*

44

of that *"playful, toying"* attitude in her voice now. *Jumping up)* No, goddamnit, we'll talk about it now! I'm not going to sit around a hotel room half the night waiting to hear how my life is going to come out . . . If you've got something to say, then have the decency to say it before you walk out that door.

> (*There is a moment's silence while each tries to compose himself . . .* SAM *turns back into the the room and closes the door*)

SAM   . . . Is there any coffee left?

KAREN   It's that bad, huh? . . . All right, sit down, I'll get you some coffee. (*She starts to cross to the table and stops, looking at her hands.* SAM *crosses to the sofa. He puts down his attaché case by the coffee table and sits*) Look at this. I'm shaking like a leaf. Pour it yourself. I have a feeling in a few minutes I'm not going to be too crazy about you.

> (KAREN *crosses and sits on the ottoman next to the sofa, hands clasped together.* SAM *finds it difficult to look at her*)

SAM   . . . No matter what, Karen, in twenty-three years my feelings for you have never changed. You're my wife, I still love you.

KAREN   Oh, God, am I in trouble.

SAM   It has nothing to do with you. It's something that just happened . . . It's true, I am having an affair with her . . . (SAM *waits for* KAREN *to react. She merely sits and looks at her hands*) . . . It's been going on for about six months now . . . I tried stopping it a few times, it didn't work . . . After a couple of days I'd start it again . . . And then—well, what's the point in going on with this? You wanted honesty, I'm giving it to you. I'm having an affair with Jean, that's all there is to it.

KAREN (*Looks up*) Who's Jean?

SAM Jean! Miss McCormack.

KAREN Oh. For a minute I thought there were two of them.

SAM I'm not very good at this. I don't know what I'm supposed to say now.

KAREN Don't worry about it. You're doing fine. (*She gets up and moves to the table*) You want that coffee now? I just stopped shaking.

SAM . . . What are we going to do?

KAREN (*Turns back to* SAM) Well, you're taken care of. You're having an affair. I'm the one who needs an activity.

SAM Karen, I'll do whatever you want.

KAREN Whatever *I* want?

SAM I'll leave. I'll get out tonight . . . Or I'll stop seeing her. I'll get rid of her in the office. I'll try it any way you want.

KAREN (*Moves to the sofa*) Oh. Okay. I choose "Stop Seeing Jean" . . . Gee, that was easy. (*Snaps her fingers*) Now we can go back to our old normal life and live happily ever after. (*Starts to pour coffee, but stops and puts the pot down*) It's not my day. Even the coffee's cold.

SAM Oh, come on, Karen, don't play "Aren't we civilized." Call me a bastard. Throw the coffee at me.

KAREN You're a bastard. You want cream and sugar?

SAM It's funny how our attitudes have suddenly changed. What happened to "I think a man of your age *should* have an affair"?

KAREN It looked good in the window but terrible when I got it home.

SAM If it's any solace to you, I never thought it would go this far. I don't even remember how it started . . .

KAREN Think, it'll come back to you.

SAM Do you know she worked for me for two years and I never batted an eye at her?

KAREN Good for you, Sam.

SAM (*Angry*) Oh, come on.
(*Crosses to the bedroom and stretches out across the bed*)

KAREN (*She follows him into the bedroom*) No, Sam, I want to hear about it. She worked for you for two years and you didn't know her first name was Jean. And then one night you were both working late, and suddenly you let down your hair and took off your glasses and she said, "Why, Mr. Nash, you're beautiful" . . .

SAM (*Takes a pillow and places it over his head*) That's it, word for word. You must have been hiding in the closet.

KAREN (*Tears the pillow away and throws it back down on the bed*) All right, you want to know when I think the exact date your crummy little affair started? I'll tell you. It was June nineteenth. It was your birthday, and you just turned fifty years old. Five-oh, count

47

'em, folks, and you were feeling good and sorry for yourself. Right?

SAM   Oh, God, here comes Doctor Franzblau again.

KAREN   And the only reason you picked on Miss Mc-Cormack was because she was probably the first one you saw that morning . . . If she was sick that day, this affair very well could have been with your elevator operator.

SAM   Wrong. He's fifty-two and I don't go for older men.

KAREN *(Breaks away and crosses to the living room)*   You were right before, Sam. Let's discuss this later tonight.

SAM *(Sitting up on his side on the bed)*   No, no. We've opened this up, let's bring it all out. I've told you the truth, I'm involved with another woman. I'm not proud of it, Karen, but those are the facts. Now what am I supposed to do about it?

KAREN *(Moves back to the bedroom doorway)*   Well, I *would* suggest committing suicide, but I'm afraid you might think I meant *me* . . . *(Goes back to the living room)* I have one other suggestion. Forget it.

SAM *(Sharply)*   Forget it?

KAREN *(Pacing above the sofa)*   I understand it, Sam. It's not your fault. But maybe I can live with it until it's over. What else can I do, Sam, I'm attached to you. So go out, have a good time tonight and when you come home, bring me the *Daily News,* I'm getting sick of the *Post.*
    (Sits on the sofa)

SAM   If I lived with you another twenty-three years, I don't think I'd ever understand you.

48

KAREN   If that's a proposition, I accept.

SAM   (*Gets up and moves to* KAREN)   Damn it, Karen, stop accepting everything in life that's thrown at you. Fight back once in a while. Don't understand me. Hate me! I am *not* going through a middle-aged adjustment. I'm having an affair. A cheating, sneaking, sordid affair.

KAREN   If it helps you to romanticize it, Sam, all right. I happen to know better.

SAM   (*Crossing above the sofa to the fireplace*)   You don't know better at all. You didn't even know I was having an affair.

KAREN   I suspected it. You were working three nights a week and we weren't getting any richer.

SAM   (*Leaning on the mantelpiece*)   I see. And now that you know the truth I have your blessings.

KAREN   No, just my permission. I'm your wife, not your mother.

SAM   That's indecent. I never heard such a thing in my life. For crying out loud, Karen, I'm losing all respect for you.

KAREN   What's the matter, Sam, am I robbing you of all those delicious guilt feelings? Will you feel better if I go to pieces and try to lash back at you?

SAM   (*Crosses below the sofa*)   At least I would understand it. It's normal. I don't know why you're not having hysterics and screaming for a lawyer.

KAREN   (*Getting up to confront him*)   All right, Sam, if it'll make you happier . . . I think you stink. You're a vain, self-pitying, deceiving, ten-pound box of rancid no-cal cottage cheese. How'm I doing?

SAM Swell. Now we're finally getting somewhere.

KAREN Oh, you like this, don't you? It makes everything nice and simple for you. Now you can leave here the martyred, misunderstood husband. Well, I won't give you the satisfaction. I take it back, Sam. (*Sits on the sofa. Pleasantly, with great control*) You're a pussycat. I'll have milk and cookies for you when you get home.

SAM (*Sits on the ottoman*) No, no. Finish what you were saying. Get it off your chest, Karen. It's been building up for twenty-three years. I want to hear everything. Vain, self-pitying, what else? Go on, what else?

KAREN You're adorable. Eat your heart out.

SAM (*Furious*) Karen, don't do this to me.

KAREN I'm sorry, I'm a forgiving woman. I can't help myself.

SAM (*Gets up, takes his case and crosses to the door*) You're driving me right out of here, you know that, don't you?

KAREN There'll always be room for you in my garage.

SAM If I walk out this door now, I don't come back.

KAREN I think you will.

SAM What makes you so sure?

KAREN You forgot to take your eye drops.
      (SAM *storms to the coffee table, snatches up the drops and crosses back to the door. He stops*)

SAM Before I go I just want to say one thing. Whatever you think of me is probably true. No, not probably, *definitely*. I have been a bastard right from the beginning. I don't expect you to forgive me.

KAREN But I do.

SAM (*Whirling back to her*) Let me finish. I don't expect you to forgive me. But I ask you with all conscience, with all your understanding, not to blame Jean for any of this.

KAREN (*Collapses on the couch. Then pulling herself together*) I'll send her a nice gift.

SAM (*Puts down his case beside the sofa*) She's been torturing herself ever since this started. *I'm* the one who forced the issue.

KAREN (*Moving away from him on the sofa, mimics JEAN*) "It didn't show up on the 1400 but I rechecked it with my own files and made the correction on the 640" . . . You know as well as I do that's code for "I'll meet you at the Picadilly Hotel."

SAM (*Kneeling beside the sofa*) You won't believe me, will you? That she's a nice girl.

KAREN Nice for you and nice for me are two different things.

SAM If it's that Sunday supplement psychology you're using, Karen, it's backfiring, because you're just making it easier for me.

KAREN Well, you like things easy, don't you? You don't even have an affair the hard way.

SAM Meaning what?

KAREN (*Getting up*) Meaning you could have at least taken the trouble to look outside your office for a girl . . . (*Picks up an imaginary phone*) "Miss McCormack, would you please come inside and take an affair!" . . . Honestly, Sam.
(*Moves above the sofa*)

SAM Karen, don't force me to say nice things about her to you.

KAREN I can't help it. I'm just disappointed in you. It's so damned unoriginal.

SAM What did you want her to be, a fighter pilot with the Israeli air force?

KAREN *Everyone* cheats with their secretary. I expected more from *my* husband!

SAM (*Shaking his head*) I never saw you like this. You live with a person your whole life, you don't really know them.

KAREN (*Crossing below the sofa to the bedroom*) Go on, Sam, go have your affair. You're fifty-one years old. In an hour it may be too late.
(*Sits at the dresser and brushes her hair*)

SAM (*Getting up and crossing to her in the bedroom*) By God, you are something. You are really something special, Karen. Twenty-three years I'm married to you and I still can't make you out. You don't look much different than the ordinary woman, but I promise you there is nothing walking around on two legs that compares in any way, shape or form to the likes of you.

KAREN (*Drops the brush and turns to him. Laughing*)

. . . So if I'm so special, what are you carrying on with secretaries for?

SAM   I'll be goddamned if I know . . .
        (*They look at each other. He turns and starts to the front door, taking his attaché case*)

KAREN (*Following him into the living room*)   Sam! (SAM *stops*) Sam . . . do I still have my two choices? (*He turns and looks at her*) Because if I do . . . I choose "Get rid of Miss McCormack." (*He looks away*) I pick "Stay here and work it out with me, Sam." (KAREN *turns her back to him and leans against the arm of the sofa*) . . . Because the other way I think I'm going to lose. Don't go to the office tonight, Sam . . . Stay with me . . . Please.

SAM (*Leaning on the console table, he looks at her*)   I swear, I wish we could go back the way it was before. A couple of years ago, before there were any problems.

KAREN   Maybe we can, Sam. We'll do what you said before. We'll lie. We'll tell each other everything is all right . . . There is nothing wrong in the office tonight, there is no Miss McCormack and I'm twenty-seven goddamned years old . . . What do you say, Sam?

SAM (*Moves about indecisively*)   . . . Maybe tomorrow, Karen . . . I can't—tonight! I'll—I'll see you.

KAREN   When? (*He exits, leaving the door open*) Never mind. I love surprises.
        (*As SAM leaves, the WAITER appears with a tray with an ice bucket filled with a bottle of champagne and two glasses*)

WAITER   The champagne . . . I brought two glasses just

in case. (*He closes the door and places the ice bucket and glasses on the desk. He glances back*) Is he coming back?

KAREN (*Remains leaning on the sofa*) ... Funny you should ask that.
(*He begins to open the bottle*)

Curtain

Visitor from Hollywood

*Suite 719 at the Plaza. It is about three in the afternoon
on a warm, sunny spring day.*

The WAITER *is just finishing setting up some fresh
glasses and bottles of liquor on top of the bureau between
the windows in the living room.*

The telephone in the bedroom rings. JESSE KIPLINGER
emerges from the bathroom. JESSE *is about forty, a con-
fident, self-assured man. He is applying after-shave lotion
to his face. He is dressed in "Hollywood mod," with a tan
turtleneck sweater and tight blue suede pants. His shoes
are highly polished and buckled. He has the latest-style
haircut, with bangs falling over his forehead. He crosses to
the phone and picks it up.*

JESSE Hello? . . . Oh, just a minute. (*He drops the
phone and crosses to the* WAITER) I'll take that. (*He
indicates the check, which the* WAITER *hands him. He
signs it and returns it to the* WAITER, *who nods and
crosses to the door.* JESSE *picks up the phone and holds
his hand over the phone until the* WAITER *is gone,
closing the door behind him. Then into the phone*)
Put her on . . . (*Waits, then in a much softer, roman-
tically persuasive tone*) Hello? . . . Muriel? Where
are you? . . . Well, come on up . . . Yes, I'm positive
it's all right . . . (*More insistently*) . . . Muriel, do you
want me to come down and get you? . . . All right,
then, take the elevator and come to Suite 719 . . .
And stop being so silly, I'm dying to see you. (*He
hangs up, thinks a second, then picks up the phone
again*) Hello, operator? This is Mr. Kiplinger in Suite

719. Would you please hold all local calls for the next hour, I'm going to be in conference . . . (*Checks an appointment book on the night table*) Make that an hour and a half . . . Thank you. (*He hangs up and begins to clear the bed of a collection of scripts, trade papers and galley proofs. Kneeling, he pushes them under the bed. Rising, he carefully smoothes the spread. He snatches up a section of colored comics from the arm of the armchair and throws it into the waste-basket. Taking a blue button-down sweater from the back of a chair at the dresser, he puts it on with a great flair and carefully examines himself in the mirror on the closet door. Satisfied with his appearance, he crosses to the living room and checks the bar set-up on the bureau. The front doorbell rings.* JESSE *crosses to answer it, checking his hair in the mirror over the mantel as he does. He is finally ready. Taking a deep breath, he opens the door.* MURIEL TATE *stands there.* MURIEL *is in her late thirties and is extremely attractive. She wears a bright-yellow spring coat and a simple, demure, high-necked gray dress which shows off her svelte, still girlish figure. Her hair falls simply to her shoulders, held back by a wide white band.* MURIEL *is a warm, easy, smiling woman who seems as naïve and vulnerable as the day she graduated from Tenafly High School. When the door opens, the two of them greet each other with enormous smiles.* JESSE *throws out his arms*) Muriel!

MURIEL (*Smiles, cocks her head*) Jesse?

JESSE It's not.

MURIEL It is.

JESSE Muriel, I can't believe it. Is it really you?

MURIEL   It's me, Muriel.

JESSE   Well, come on in, for pete's sakes, come on in.

MURIEL   (*Enters with a rush and crosses to the far side of the sofa*)   I can only stay for a few minutes.

JESSE   (*Closes the door and follows her to below the near side of the sofa*)   My God, it's good to see you. (*They stand and confront each other*)

MURIEL   I just dropped in to say hello. I really can't stay.

JESSE   You sounded good on the phone, but you look even better.

MURIEL   Because I've got to get back to New Jersey. I'm parked in a one-hour zone. Hello, Jesse, I think I'm very nervous.

JESSE   Hey! Hello, Muriel.

MURIEL   Same old Muriel, heh?

JESSE   What do you mean, same old Muriel? You look fantastic (*Arms outstretched, he moves to her*) Come here, let me take a good look at you.

MURIEL   (*Evading him, crosses below the coffee table*) Oh, don't, Jesse. Don't look at me. I've been stuck in the Holland Tunnel for two hours. What time is it? Tell me when it's three o'clock. I can't stay.
(*Sits in the armchair*)

JESSE   (*Moves toward her*)   Muriel, I can't get over it. You look absolutely wonderful.

MURIEL   Well, I *feel* absolutely wonderful.

JESSE   (*Sitting on the arm of the sofa*)   I really, sincerely mean that. You simply look incredibly fantastic.

MURIEL   Well, I *feel* incredibly fantastic.

JESSE   Well, you look it.

MURIEL   Well, I *feel* it.

JESSE   And how are you?

MURIEL (*Without enthusiasm*)   I'm all right . . . I don't know why I'm so nervous, do you?
   (*She shrugs her coat off her shoulders and arranges it over the back of the chair*)

JESSE   No. I can't imagine why you should be so nervous.

MURIEL   Neither can I. I just am . . . Should I be here?

JESSE   Why not? Is there anything wrong in it?

MURIEL   Oh, no. No, of course not. There's nothing wrong in it. My God, no. I don't see anything wrong. I just dropped by from New Jersey to say hello. What's wrong with that? . . . I just don't think I should be here. (*Getting up and moving toward the mantel*) Is it three o'clock yet?

JESSE (*Moving toward her*)   Little Muriel Tate, all grown up and married. How many kids you got now?

MURIEL   Three.

JESSE   No kidding? Three kids . . . What are they?

MURIEL   A boy and a girl.

JESSE   A boy and a girl?

MURIEL (*Breaking away to the other side of the sofa*)   And another boy who's away in camp. I can't even think straight. Isn't this terrible?

JESSE (*Moving to the sofa. Good-naturedly*) What's wrong?

MURIEL I don't know, I can't catch my breath. Well, it's *you*, that's the simple explanation. I'm nervous about meeting you.

JESSE Me? Me? Jesse Kiplinger, your high school boy friend from Tenafly, New Jersey. Ohh, Muriel.

MURIEL You know what I mean, Mr. "Famous Hollywood Producer" staying at the Plaza Hotel.

JESSE Mr. Famous Hollywood Producer. (*Sitting on the sofa*) Muriel, you know me better than that. I haven't changed. I made a couple of pictures, that's all.

MURIEL (*Moving to the sofa*) A couple of pictures? The Easter show at the Radio City Music Hall? I stood on line with my children for three hours in the rain.

JESSE What did you do that for? You could have called my office in New York. My girl would have gotten you right in. Any time you want to see one of my pictures . . .

MURIEL Oh, I couldn't do that.

JESSE Why not?

MURIEL I couldn't. I couldn't impose like that.

JESSE You're *not* imposing.

MURIEL I am.

JESSE I *want* you to.

MURIEL What's the number?

JESSE I'll give it to you before you go. (*Getting up*)

61

But first you're going to sit down and have a drink. There's a million things I'm dying to ask you.

MURIEL Oh, no drinks for me.

JESSE One little drink.

MURIEL No, no, no. You go ahead and have a drink. I have a five-o'clock hairdresser's appointment.

JESSE You don't drink?

MURIEL Oh, once in a great while. Anyway, I've got to get home. I shouldn't even be in the city. The kids will be home from school soon and I've got to make dinner for Larry and I haven't even done my shopping in Bonwit's. No, no, I just dropped by to say hello.

JESSE What'll you have?

MURIEL A vodka stinger.

JESSE Coming right up.
        (*He crosses to the bar set-up*)

MURIEL (*Sitting on the sofa*) And then I've got to go . . . Whoooo, I finally took a breath. That felt good.

JESSE (*Pouring liquor into a shaker*) Will you relax? Will you, Muriel? Come on now. I want you to stop being so silly and relax.

MURIEL (*Chiding*) Is that how you talk to your stars when they're nervous? Is that what you say to Elke Sommer?

JESSE I don't talk to the stars. I have directors for that . . . . For God's sakes, Muriel, what are you so nervous about?

62

MURIEL Oooh, there's that famous Hollywood temper I read about . . . You want me to be frank?

JESSE Please.

MURIEL I feel funny sitting here drinking in a hotel room . . . I mean, I'm a married woman.

JESSE (*Having finished making and pouring drinks, he moves to her*) Would you feel better if we had our drinks down in the Palm Court?

MURIEL We're here, we might as well stay.

JESSE (*Handing her the drink*) Okay. Then will you sit back and relax?
　　　(*Sits down next to her on the sofa*)

MURIEL Just for a few minutes. I've got a six-o'clock hairdresser's appointment.

JESSE I thought it was at five?

MURIEL It's flexible . . . Is it warm in here?
　　　(*Putting down her drink on the coffee table*)

JESSE Why don't you take off your gloves?

MURIEL (*Shaking a finger at him*) Oh, no! Let's not have any of *that*, Mr. Jesse Kiplinger of Hollywood, California . . . My gloves will stay where they belong, if you please.

JESSE (*Putting his drink down on the coffee table*) Muriel, you are delightfully and incredibly unchanged. How long has it been now? Fifteen, sixteen years?

MURIEL Since our last date? It'll be seventeen years on August sixth.

JESSE You remembered that?

MURIEL I still have the swizzle sticks from Tavern on the Green.

JESSE (*Leaning toward her*) No, time hasn't changed you, Muriel. You're still so fresh and clean. (*Sniffs about her*) You even smell the same way.

MURIEL Ohhh?

JESSE (*Sniffs her ear*) Like cool peppermint . . . Clear, cool peppermint.

MURIEL (*Pushes his nose away with her finger*) Now, you and your nose just behave yourself . . . I did not come to the Plaza Hotel to be smelled.

JESSE And now you've blossomed and matured . . . only in reverse . . . You look younger and fresher and . . . well, you know what I mean. I just think you look absolutely fantastic.

MURIEL (*Pulls herself together. Clears her throat. Very businesslike*) You going to be in New York long, Jesse?

JESSE Possibly just till the weekend. I've got to sign a director for my new picture.

MURIEL John Huston?

JESSE Yes. How did you know that?

MURIEL Oh, we keep up on things in Tenafly . . . Mr. Famous Hollywood Producer, staying at the Plaza Hotel, signing up John Huston for his next picture.
(*Playfully pushing his leg*)

JESSE I might stay over another few days. It depends . . . on what develops.
(*He looks down at his leg. She gets up nervously*)

MURIEL   I've never been in the Plaza before. It's beautiful. (*Stops near the door to the bedroom, which is opened*) What's in there?

JESSE   The bedroom. You can go in.

MURIEL   (*Shying away, moves back to the sofa*)   It's all right, I take your word for it . . . Is this where you meet with John Huston? I mean, does he sit in here and the two of you talk and then he signs the contract? Is that how you do it?

JESSE   (*Lolling back on the sofa*)   In this very room . . . Will you stop with the celebrity routine. Aside from a couple of extra pounds, I'm still the same boy who ran anchor on the Tenafly track team.

MURIEL   And is living in the old Humphrey Bogart house in Beverly Hills.

JESSE   How did you know that?

MURIEL   (*Moving to the ottoman*)   Never mind, I know, I know . . . Maybe I haven't seen you in seventeen years, but I know an awful lot about you, Mr. Jesse Kiplinger . . . (*Sits*) Pootch!

JESSE   Pootch?

MURIEL   Isn't that what they call you in Hollywood? Your nickname? Pootch?

JESSE   Gootch!

MURIEL   I thought it was Pootch.

JESSE   No. No, no, it's Gootch.

MURIEL   I thought I read that you have all your shirts specially made by Pucci in Florence, so they call you Pootch.

JESSE   No, no. I have all my shoes made by Gucci in Rome so they call me Gootch.

MURIEL   Oh.

JESSE   (*Deprecatingly*)   It's a silly thing. I don't know why they print stories like that.

MURIEL   Because people like me like to read them. Are those Gucci shoes you're wearing now, Gootch?

JESSE   These? (*To display his shoes, he puts one foot up on the coffee table, the other over the arm of the sofa*) No. These are the one pair I had made in England. You can't get this leather in Italy. No, I have a man in Bond Street makes them for me . . . MacCombs.
> (MURIEL *reacts to the sight of his widespread legs and turns away in embarrassment*)

MURIEL   (*Attempting to make a joke*)   Well, they're beautiful shoes, *MacCootch!*

JESSE   MacCootch! That's very good. (*He laughs*) Hey, can we stop talking about me for a while?

MURIEL   (*Turns back to him*)   Why? I think you're very interesting to talk about.

JESSE   Well, I don't. I'm very bored with me. I'm much more interested in you . . . (*Sits up and hands her a drink*) But first let's have our drinks.

MURIEL   And then I've got to go.
> (*Takes the glass*)

JESSE   Let's say, to renewing old acquaintances.

MURIEL   You drink to that. (*Moves to the sofa*) I'll

drink to your new picture winning the Academy Award.

JESSE   Muriel, it's not going to win the Academy Award. It's not even going to get nominated. (*Beginning to laugh*) As a matter of fact, it's a piece of crap . . . (*Catches himself*) Excuse me, Muriel.

MURIEL   (*Sitting on the sofa*)   Be that as it may, it's going to gross over nine million. Domestic.

JESSE   That's beside the point . . . How did you know that?

MURIEL   I know, I know, Mr. "Gootch" Kiplinger . . . I've been following your career very closely, if you please.

JESSE   (*Moving closer*)   Muriel, it is so exciting seeing you again. The minute you walked in that door, I got a—a tingle, all over, the way I used to . . . You know what I mean.

MURIEL   (*Trying to remain matter-of-fact*)   I'm sure I don't. I have three children and I'm very happy and I have a wonderful life and I have no business being in a hotel room in New York at three o'clock in the afternoon with a man I haven't seen since Tavern on the Green seventeen years ago. (*He kisses her on the lips. She looks at him*)—Any particular reason you did that?

JESSE   (*Still leaning toward her*)   I wanted to. Desperately.

MURIEL   Do you always blithely go ahead and do whatever you want to?

JESSE   If I can get away with it . . . As a matter of fact

. . . if you don't object too strenuously, I'm going to kiss you again.

MURIEL   ...And then I've got to go. (JESSE *kisses her again tenderly on the lips. She lets him kiss her for a moment. Then jumps up and moves away*) Woo...That'll be enough of that, Mr. Do-Whatever-You-Want-to Kiplinger. Wow, that vodka stinger has really gone to my head.

JESSE   (*Noncommittally*)   It's even better when you drink it.

MURIEL   (*Takes her drink from the coffee table and crosses to the chair*)   Now, don't confuse me. I'm nervous enough as it is. Cheers. (*Drinks*) Was it good?

JESSE   (*Taking his drink*)   What? The drink?

MURIEL   The kiss.

JESSE   The kiss? Yes, the kiss was very good.

MURIEL   What did it feel like?

JESSE   What do you mean, what did it feel like?

MURIEL   (*Sitting in the chair*)   Was it a good kiss or a medium kiss or a waste-of-time kiss? I'm interested in knowing your reaction.

JESSE   Why? You never asked me that when I kissed you in Tenafly.

MURIEL   You weren't a famous Hollywood producer living in Humphrey Bogart's house signing John Huston for your next picture in Tenafly. Can I please have your reaction to my kiss?

JESSE   It was a superb kiss.

Photo Credit: *Martha Swope*

Maureen Stapleton as Muriel Tate
George C. Scott as Jess Kiplinger
"Visitor From Hollywood"

MURIEL (*Puts her drink down on the floor next to the chair. Takes a compact from her purse on the chair*) It wasn't superb. I don't kiss superbly. It was an average, inexperienced, everyday New Jersey kiss . . . I don't know why I let you kiss me anyway, "Mr. Famous Hollywood Kisser."
(*Powdering her face*)

JESSE (*Smiles warmly*) Is it possible that you are the last, sweet, simple, unchanged, unspoiled woman living in the world today?

MURIEL I'm sure I don't know what you're talking about. (*Looking in the compact mirror*) Oh, God, look at my lips. I'd never get past the house detective. What time is it?

JESSE (*Looks at his watch*) Twenty after.

MURIEL Three? Already? I've got to go.
(*Puts the compact back in her purse, gets up and begins to gather her purse and coat from the chair*)

JESSE Not yet.

MURIEL I must.

JESSE Ten more minutes?

MURIEL I can't . . .

JESSE Please!

MURIEL I'll stay five.
(*Sits back down in the chair*)

JESSE Good.

MURIEL Why did you call me yesterday?

JESSE (*Smiles*) I called you because, believe it or not, I've been thinking about you.

MURIEL For seventeen years?

JESSE On and off.

MURIEL In Humphrey Bogart's old house? I don't believe you, "Mr. International Liar." And I don't trust you. (*She gets up and again begins to gather her belongings*) And I'm not staying.

JESSE (*Quietly*) Good-by.

MURIEL (*Stops in surprise*) Do you mean that?

JESSE I don't want to force you to stay here. You know what's best for you.

MURIEL (*Looks at him*) I'll just finish my drink.
(*She puts her things back on the chair and picks up her drink*)

JESSE Muriel, you must believe me when I tell you I have no ulterior motives in asking you here today. I just wanted to see you. I'm trying to impress you with the fact that you are the only, solitary, real, honest-to-goodness, unphoney woman that I have been with since the day I arrived in Hollywood seventeen years ago.

MURIEL What about your mother?

JESSE She's the worst one.

MURIEL (*Sitting next to him on the sofa*) Well, your mother must be very proud to have such a famous son.

JESSE (*Edges closer to her*) Do you know, in my own quiet way, I was crazy about you?

MURIEL (*Puts the drink down on the table*) As a matter of fact, everyone in Tenafly is proud of you. Even Larry, my husband, talks about you all the time. He always says, "Jesse Kiplinger, Jesse Kiplinger, that's all I ever hear around this house."

    (*Stops and thinks about what she has just said*)

JESSE I remember exactly what you looked like the day I left for California. You were wearing a tan raincoat, a tweed skirt and a brown sweater. And a little locket that your grandmother had given you. (*Traces a locket on her chest*) Do you remember?

MURIEL I remember when your first picture came to Tenafly, that's what I remember. Everybody went. Do you know it was the only Jeff Chandler picture that ever played two weeks at the Hillside Drive-In?

JESSE Even then, you had a quality about you, Muriel, that was sort of—well, untouched. (*Puts his hand on the outside of her leg and caresses her*) You were the only girl that gave me pleasure in just holding her hand.

MURIEL (*Determinedly ignoring* JESSE's *actions*) You know a lot of the girls from school still kid me about you. I mean when they see your name in a column or something like that.

JESSE I didn't expect to see it any more, Muriel, that quality of honesty . . . and frankness . . . that ability to cut through deceit (*Moves his hand, and going underneath her skirt, puts it between her legs*) and phoniness with just one look through those big, unsuspecting, wide-open eyes. I really did not expect to see it again in my lifetime.

MURIEL They always kid me and say, oh, if I married you instead of Larry, I'd be living in Hollywood now, going to parties with James Garner and Otto Preminger, running around with the Rat Pack.

JESSE You don't know what you are. You really don't . . . Well, I'll tell you what you are. You're something very special. I *know,* Muriel.

MURIEL . . . I mean I wouldn't even know what to say to Otto Preminger.

JESSE Don't change, Muriel. Don't ever change the sweet, simple way you are.
(*He kisses her neck, deeply. For a minute she is lost in the embrace and then, without changing her mood*)

MURIEL Do you know Frank Sinatra?

JESSE (*Slowly comes out of her neck and looks at her*) Who?

MURIEL Frank Sinatra. Did you ever meet him?

JESSE (*Slightly shaken, pulls back, takes his hand away and sits back on the sofa*) Yes. Yes, I know Frank.

MURIEL What's he like?

JESSE Frank? . . . I . . . I don't really know him that well, we had dinner a few times.

MURIEL Where? In his house?

JESSE Once in a restaurant, once I think in his house. I don't remember.

MURIEL Was Mia there?

JESSE Uh . . . no. This was before he met Mia.

72

MURIEL   So in other words, you never met Mia?

JESSE   Yes, I did meet Mia, but she wasn't married to Frank then.

MURIEL   I see. They say he's very generous. Is that true? Is he as generous as they say?

JESSE   Yeah, I guess so. He served very large portions . . . I don't know. Christ, who cares about Frank Sinatra?

MURIEL   (*Hurt*)   I'm sorry—I was just curious. I didn't mean to pry into your personal life. Well, I've got to be going.
     (*She gets up and moves to the chair*)

JESSE   (*Apologetic*)   Wait, Muriel . . .

MURIEL   (*Getting her belongings from the chair*)   No, I've got to leave before the traffic starts. If I get stuck in the Holland Tunnel again and I'm late for Larry's dinner, he'll want to know where I was, and I don't lie very well, and oh, God, I don't know why I came here in the first place . . . (*Drops her things back in the chair. Becoming more and more upset*) What have I done?

JESSE   You haven't done anything, Muriel.

MURIEL   (*Pacing*)   Haven't done anything? I'm sitting there letting you kiss me and smell me . . .

JESSE   Muriel, if I've done anything to offend you, I'm sorry.

MURIEL   (*Moving toward the windows*)   I must have been out of my mind, coming to the Plaza Hotel in the middle of the week.

73

JESSE   There is no reason to get yourself upset. I didn't do anything worse than give you a friendly kiss.

MURIEL   (*Coming back to the sofa*) I happen to enjoy a wonderful reputation.

JESSE   I'm glad you enjoy it . . . Now stop being so silly. Sit down and finish your drink.

MURIEL   I suppose you'll go back to Hollywood and have a big laugh with Otto Preminger over this.

JESSE   I wouldn't dream of it.

MURIEL   Promise.

JESSE   I promise.

MURIEL   Say it. Say, "I will not have a big laugh with Otto Preminger over this."

JESSE   I don't even *talk* to Otto Preminger. Why would I laugh at you? I have nothing but respect and the warmest of feelings for you.

MURIEL   You do? God's truth?

JESSE   God's truth. You're an angel.

MURIEL   Really? (*She hesitates a moment, then sits on the arm of the sofa*) Would I fit in with your crowd?

JESSE   No, you would not fit in with my crowd. You're too good for them. You're too sweet and honest for the whole slimy bunch.

MURIEL   . . . But which ones would I fit in with?

JESSE   Muriel, I don't know what kind of distorted image you have of these people, but they're not what you think they are. *I'm* not what you think I am. All these things you read in the paper about me being witty, charming, the boy genius, that's only part of the story. Do you know what kind of a life I really lead in Hollywood?

MURIEL   Are you going to tell me?

JESSE   Yes, I'll tell you. Why did I call you yesterday? After seventeen years? Okay, let's start with, "Yes, I'm a Famous Hollywood Producer. Yes, I never made a picture that lost money. Yes, I got that magic touch, call it talent, whatever you want, I don't know" . . . The fact is, ever since I was old enough to sneak into the Ridgewood Theatre in Tenafly, I've been a movie nut. (*Getting up, stands by the sofa*) Not only have I seen every Humphrey Bogart movie he ever made at least eight times, I now own a print of all those pictures. Why do you think I was so crazy to buy his house? (*Moves slowly to the window*) . . . So I went to Hollywood and was very lucky and extremely smart and presto, I became a producer. (*Unobtrusively pulls down the shade*) I love making movies. Some are good, some are bad, most of them are fun. I hope I can continue doing it for the next fifty years. That's one half of my life. The other half is that in the last fourteen years I've been married three times—to three of the worst bitches you'd ever want to meet.
(*Gets a bottle of vodka and a glass from the bar*)

MURIEL   Jesse, you don't have to tell me any of this if you don't want to.

JESSE   Maybe you're right. (*Moves to the front door and locks it*) Maybe I shouldn't be telling you about my sordid Hollywood past.
(*Leans on the mantel*)

MURIEL (*Settling down on the sofa, she picks up her drink*) . . . So you married these three bitches, then what happened?

JESSE (*Moves to* MURIEL) What happened . . . I gave them love, I gave them a home, I gave them a beautiful way of life—and the three bitches took me for every cent I got. (*Refills her glass, then sits on the floor by the armchair*) But I don't even care about the money, screw it—excuse me, Muriel. What hurts is that they took the guts out of me. They were phony, unfaithful, all of them. Did you know I caught my first wife, Dolores, in bed with a jockey? A jockey! (*Indicates the man's size, holding his hand a foot off the floor*) Do you know what it does to a man's self-respect to find his wife in the sack with a four-foot-eight shrimp, weighs a hundred and twelve pounds? But as I said before, screw it. Tell me if I'm shocking you, Muriel.
(*Refills his own drink*)

MURIEL I'll let you know.
(*She drinks*)

JESSE All right . . . My second wife, Carlotta . . . She was *keeping* her Spanish guitar teacher . . . *Keeping him!* . . . I never caught her, but she didn't fool me. *No one* takes twenty-seven thousand dollars' worth of guitar lessons in one year . . .

MURIEL Is Carlotta the one you met at Kirk Douglas's house?

JESSE Yes, as a matter of fact. Was that in the paper too?

MURIEL Sheilah Graham's column. It was a big party

for the Ukrainian Folk Dancers and the Los Angeles Rams.

JESSE (*Getting up, replenishes her drink*) Muriel, forget the Los Angeles Rams...(*Putting the bottle and his glass down on the console table, he crosses behind the sofa*) Listen to what I'm saying to you. I am in a very bad way. I've been through three hellish, miserable marriages. I don't want to go that route again. I am losing my faith and belief that there is anything left that resembles an uncorrupt woman . . . (*Sighs*) So last week my mother, who still gets the Tenafly newspaper, shows me a picture of the PTA annual outing at Palisades this year, and who is there on the front page, coming in first in the Mother and Daughter Potato Race, (*Leans in to* MURIEL *over the side arm of the couch*) looking every bit as young and lovely and as sweet as she did seventeen years ago, was my last salvation...Muriel Tate. (*Gradually moving to the bedroom door*) That's why I had to see you, Muriel. Just to talk to you, to have a drink, to spend five minutes, to reaffirm my faith that there *are* decent women in this world . . . even if it's only one . . . even if you're the last of a dying species . . . if somebody like you exists, Muriel . . . then maybe there's still somebody for me . . . *That's* why I called you yesterday.
(JESSE *has finished his speech. He is somewhat spent, emotionally. He moves to the bed and sits*)

MURIEL (*Getting up and moving toward the bedroom door*) Well . . . well . . . well . . .

JESSE (*From the bedroom*) I hope whatever I said didn't embarrass you, Muriel . . . but hell, if you expect honesty from another person you can't be anything less than honest yourself.

MURIEL (*Still at the doorway*)   I'm not embarrassed, I'm flattered. To think a famous person like you wants to confide in a plain person like me . . .

JESSE (*Gets up and moves to her in the living room*)   Now you finish your vodka stinger and then I'm going to let you go.

MURIEL (*Pouring herself a drink at the bar*)   Oh, I've got plenty of time. Larry's never home till seven. (*She holds up the drink*) Cheers. (*She drinks.* JESSE *crosses to* MURIEL, *touches her*)

JESSE   How are you, Muriel? Are you happy?

MURIEL   Happy? . . . Oh, yes. I think if I'm anything, I'm happy.
(*Moves down to the sofa*)

JESSE   I'm glad. You deserve happiness, Muriel.

MURIEL   Yes, Larry and I are very happy . . . (*She drinks*) I would have to say that Larry and I have one of the happier marriages in Tenafly.
(*She drinks again*)

JESSE   That's wonderful.

MURIEL   I mean, we've had our ups and downs like any married couple, but I think in the final analysis what's left is . . . that we're happy.

JESSE (*Moves down to her*)   I couldn't be more pleased. Well, listen, it's no surprise. Larry's a wonderful guy.

MURIEL   Do you think so?

JESSE   Don't you?

MURIEL   Yes, *I* do. But no one else seems to care for him. (*Sits on the sofa*) Of course, they don't know him the way *I* do. I'm out of stinger again.
(*Holds her glass out to* JESSE)

JESSE (*Takes her glass*)   Are you sure you're going to be all right? I mean, driving?

MURIEL (*Gradually feeling the effects of the drinks, she slowly exposes a whole, new, unexpected* MURIEL)   If I had to worry about getting home every time I had three vodka stingers, I'd give up driving. (JESSE *crosses to the bar, looking back at her in puzzlement*) . . . Yes, I'd say that in spite of everything, Larry and I have worked out happiness . . . or some form of it.

JESSE   Is he doing well in business?
(*Fills her glass once again*)

MURIEL   Oh, in business you don't have to worry. In that department he's doing great. I mean, he's really got a wonderful business there . . . Of course, it was good when my father had it. (JESSE *hands her a drink*) Ooh, cheers.

JESSE (*Sitting on the arm of the sofa*)   In what department isn't he doing well?

MURIEL   He's doing well in *every* department.

JESSE   Are you sure?

MURIEL   I'm positive.

JESSE   Then I'm glad.

MURIEL   Why, what do you hear?

JESSE   I haven't heard a thing except what you're telling me.

MURIEL   Well, I'm telling you that we have a happy marriage. Are you trying to infer we don't have a happy marriage?

JESSE   No . . .

MURIEL   Well, you're wrong. We have a happy marriage. A goddamned happy marriage. (*Tries to put the glass down on the table, misses and nearly slips off the sofa*) Oh, I'm sorry. I should have had lunch.

JESSE   (*Steadies her and picks up the glass from the floor and puts it on the table*)   Shall I order down for some food?

MURIEL   No, I can't stay. Larry'll be home about five.

JESSE   I thought he comes home at seven.

MURIEL   If he comes home at all . . . Please forgive me, Jesse, I seem to be losing control of myself.

JESSE   You drank those too quickly. Didn't you have anything to eat all day?

MURIEL   Just an olive with the two stingers I had downstairs . . . I'll be all right.

JESSE   Do you want to lie down for a while?

MURIEL   What's the point? You're going back to Hollywood in a few days . . . Oh, I see what you mean . . . Oh, God, I'm sorry, Jesse, I seem to be running off at the mouth.

JESSE   (*Sits down next to her*)   What is it, Muriel? What's with you and Larry?

MURIEL   Nothing. I told you, we're very happy. We

have tiny, little differences like every normal couple, but basically we're enormously happy together. I couldn't ask for a btter life . . . (*And she throws her arms around* JESSE *and gives him a full, passionate kiss on the lips . . . then she pulls away*) . . . Oh, you shouldn't have done that, Jesse. I'm very vulnerable right now and you mustn't take advantage . . . I'm going. I've got to go.
(*Gets up and moves away*)

JESSE (*Taking her hand*) Muriel, I didn't know.

MURIEL (*Pulling away*) No, Jesse, don't.

JESSE Why didn't you let me know?

MURIEL (*Crying, crosses to the chair for her things*) Who knew you were interested? You were always at a party with the Los Angeles Rams.

JESSE I never suspected for a minute. Why didn't you write to me?

MURIEL (*Crying*) Where? I don't know where Humphrey Bogart lived. (*Rushes to* JESSE *where he sits on the sofa and throws her arms about him*) I've got to go. Let me go.

JESSE (*With his arms about her waist*) God, how I thought about you on the plane all the way to New York.

MURIEL Please, Jesse. I've got to buy something in Bonwit's and get dinner for Larry. (*He munches on her neck*) Don't bite my neck, it'll leave marks.

JESSE You're different, Muriel. I know you are. You're not like any of the others.
(*Caressing her*)

MURIEL   I'm not different, Jesse. I'm a woman. A happily married woman with normal desires and passions. Please don't rub me.
(*Pulls away from him*)

JESSE (*Reaching out for her*)   My life is empty, Muriel. Empty. But you can fill it for me. You can.
(*Gets up and moves to her*)

MURIEL (*Retreating behind the chair*)   I can't fill your life for you, Jesse, I've got to get home. Larry'll kill me.

JESSE (*Catching her hands*)   Stay! An hour. Just one hour, that's all.

MURIEL   No, no. Tomorrow I'll be alone with my regrets and you'll be out there with Dino and Groucho . . .

JESSE (*Pulling her above the sofa in the direction of the bedroom*)   One hour, Muriel. Live my life with me for one hour.

MURIEL   No, please, Jesse. I've got to pick up my lamb chops.

JESSE   One hour, Muriel. The world can change for one hour.

MURIEL (*Stopping above the sofa*)   Can it, Jesse? Can it really?

JESSE (*Moving behind her*)   It can for me, Muriel. It can for you.

MURIEL   I don't know, Jesse. I just don't know.

JESSE   All right, we'll just talk. (*Reaches around her waist from behind her, and places his hand on her*

stomach. Soothingly) No one ever got hurt just talking, did they?

MURIEL   . . . I suppose not.

JESSE   Of course they didn't.
(*Rubbing her stomach*)

MURIEL (*Under the spell of his soft voice*)   What'll
we talk about?

JESSE   Whatever you say. Whatever you want.

MURIEL   . . . Did you go to the Academy Awards dinner
last year?

JESSE (*Resignedly*)   Certainly. I go every year.

MURIEL   Oh, God, really?

JESSE   Really.
(*For a moment, they rock gently back and forth,
but slowly, almost as in a dance step, he leads her
into the bedroom*)

MURIEL   Who did you sit next to?

JESSE (*As if to a child*)   In the theatre, I sat next to
Steve McQueen on one side and Liza Minelli on the
other.

MURIEL   She's adorable, isn't she?
(*They move into the bedroom*)

JESSE   A real pixie.

MURIEL   And who did you sit with at the dinner?

JESSE (*Leading her to the bed*)   Well, let's see, at my
table there was Charlton Heston and his wife, Joseph

E. Levine, the producer, Eva Marie Saint, Marge and Gower Champion . . .

(Sits down on the side of the bed)

MURIEL   Oh, they're cute . . . All at your table?

JESSE *(Drawing her down on his knee)* All at my table. And at the next table—there was Anthony Quinn and Virna Lisi, Paul Newman and Joanne . . .
(Searches for the name)

MURIEL   Woodward . . .

JESSE   Woodward . . . *(He begins to unzip her dress)* And there was Dean Jones and Yvette Mimieux . . .

MURIEL   Together . . . ?

JESSE   Yes, together . . . *(He gently forces her back down on the bed, at the same time pulling the dress off her shoulders)* Then behind us there was Troy Donahue and Stella Stevens, Sammy Davis, Jr., and Margot Fonteyn . . .
(They are both lying on the bed. The lights have faded out)

Curtain

Visitor from Forest Hills

Suite 719 at the Plaza. It is three o'clock on a warm Saturday afternoon in spring.

The living room is bedecked with vases and baskets of flowers. In the bedroom one opened valise containing a young woman's street clothes rests on the floor. A very large box, which had held a wedding dress, rests on the luggage rack, and a man's suit lies on the bed. A fur wrap and gloves are thrown over the back of the sofa. Telegrams of congratulation and newspapers are strewn about. The suite today is being used more or less as a dressing room, since a wedding is about to occur downstairs in one of the reception rooms.

As the lights come up, NORMA HUBLEY *is at the phone in the bedroom, impatiently tapping the receiver. She is dressed in a formal cocktail dress and a large hat, looking her very best, as any woman would want to on her daughter's wedding day. But she is extremely nervous and harassed, and with good cause—as we'll soon find out.*

NORMA (*On the phone*) Hello? . . . Hello, operator? . . . Can I have the Blue Room, please . . . The Blue Room . . . Is there a Pink Room? . . . I want the Hubley-Eisler wedding . . . The Green Room, that's it. Thank you . . . Could you please hurry, operator, it's an emergency . . . (*She looks over at the bathroom nervously. She paces back and forth*) Hello? . . . Who's this? . . . Mr. Eisler . . . It's Norma Hubley . . . No, everything's fine . . . Yes, we're coming right down . . . (*She is smiling and trying to act as pleasant*

87

and as calm as possible) Yes, you're right, it certainly
is the big day . . . Mr. Eisler, is my husband there?
. . . Would you, please? . . . Oh! Well, I'd like to wish
you the very best of luck too . . . Borden's a wonderful
boy . . . Well, they're *both* wonderful kids . . . No,
no. She's as calm as a cucumber . . . That's the
younger generation, I guess . . . Yes, everything seems
to be going along beautifully . . . Absolutely beautifully . . . Oh, thank you. (*Her husband has obviously
just come on the other end, because the expression on
her face changes violently and she screams a rasping
whisper filled with doom. Sitting on the bed*) Roy?
You'd better get up here right away, we're in big
trouble . . . Don't ask questions, just get up here . . .
I hope you're not drunk because I can't handle this
alone . . . Don't say anything. Just smile and walk
leisurely out the door . . . and then get the hell up
here as fast as you can. (*She hangs up, putting the
phone back on the night table. She crosses to the
bathroom and then puts her head up against the door.
Aloud through the bathroom door*) All right, Mimsey,
your father's on his way up. Now, I want you to come
out of that bathroom and get married. (*There is no
answer*) Do you hear me? . . . I've had enough of
this nonsense . . . Unlock that door! (*That's about the
end of her authority. She wilts and almost pleads*)
Mimsey, darling, please come downstairs and get married, you know your father's temper . . . I know what
you're going through now, sweetheart, you're just
nervous . . . Everyone goes through that on their
wedding day . . . It's going to be all right, darling.
You love Borden and he loves you. You're both going
to have a wonderful future. So please come out of
the bathroom! (*She listens; there is no answer*)

Mimsey, if you don't care about your life, think about mine. Your father'll kill me. (*The front doorbell rings.* NORMA *looks off nervously and moves to the other side of the bed*) Oh, God, he's here! . . . Mimsey! Mimsey, please, spare me this . . . If you want, I'll have it annulled next week, but please come out and get married! (*There is no answer from the bathroom but the front doorbell rings impatiently*) All right, I'm letting your father in. And heaven help the three of us!

> (*She crosses through the bedroom into the living room. She crosses to the door and opens it as* ROY HUBLEY *bursts into the room.* ROY *is dressed in striped trousers, black tail coat, the works. He looks elegant but he's not too happy in this attire. He is a volatile, explosive man equipped to handle the rigors of the competitive business world, but a nervous, frightened man when it comes to the business of marrying off his only daughter*)

ROY Why are you standing here? There are sixty-eight people down there drinking my liquor. If there's gonna be a wedding, let's have a wedding. Come on! (*He starts back out the door but sees that* NORMA *is not going anywhere. She sits on the sofa. He comes back in*) . . . Didn't you hear what I said? There's another couple waiting to use the Green Room. Come on, let's go!

> (*He makes a start out again*)

NORMA (*Very calm*) Roy, could you sit down a minute? I want to talk to you about something.

ROY (*She must be mad*) You want to talk *now*? You had twenty-one years to talk while she was growing up. I'll talk to you when they're in Bermuda. Can we please have a wedding?

NORMA We can't have a wedding until you and I have a talk.

ROY Are you crazy? While you and I are talking here, there are four musicians playing downstairs for seventy dollars an hour. I'll talk to you later when we're dancing. Come on, get Mimsey and let's go.
(*He starts out again*)

NORMA That's what I want to talk to you about.

ROY (*Comes back*) Mimsey?

NORMA Sit down. You're not going to like this.

ROY Is she sick?

NORMA She's not sick . . . exactly.

ROY What do you mean, she's not sick exactly? Either she's sick or she's not sick. Is she sick?

NORMA She's not sick.

ROY Then let's have a wedding! (*He crosses into the bedroom*) Mimsey, there's two hundred dollars' worth of cocktail frankfurters getting cold downstairs . . . (*He looks around the empty room*) Mimsey? (*He crosses back to the living room to the side of the sofa. He looks at* NORMA) . . . Where's Mimsey?

NORMA Promise you're not going to blame me.

ROY Blame you for what? What did you do?

NORMA I didn't do anything. But I don't want to get blamed for it.

ROY   What's going on here? Are you going to tell me where Mimsey is?

NORMA   Are you going to take an oath you're not going to blame me?

ROY   *I take it! I take it!* NOW WHERE THE HELL IS SHE?

NORMA   . . . She's locked herself in the bathroom. She's not coming out and she's not getting married.
(ROY *looks at* NORMA *incredulously. Then, because it must be an insane joke, he smiles at her. There is even the faint glint of a chuckle*)

ROY (*Softly*)   . . . No kidding, where is she?

NORMA (*Turns away*)   He doesn't believe me. I'll kill myself.
(ROY *turns and storms into the bedroom. He crosses to the bathroom and knocks on the door. Then he tries it. It's locked. He tries again. He bangs on the door with his fist*)

ROY   Mimsey? . . . Mimsey? . . . MIMSEY? (*There is no reply. Girding himself, he crosses back through the bedroom into the living room to the sofa. He glares at* NORMA) . . . All right, what did you say to her?

NORMA (*Jumping up and moving away*)   I knew it! I knew you'd blame me. You took an oath. God'll punish you.

ROY   I'm not blaming you. I just want to know what *stupid* thing you said to her that made her do this.

NORMA   I didn't say a word. I was putting on my lipstick, she was in the bathroom, I heard the door go click, it was locked, my whole life was over, what do you want from me?

ROY   And you didn't say a word?

NORMA   Nothing.

ROY   (*Ominously moving toward her as* NORMA *backs away*)   I see. In other words, you're trying to tell me that a normal, healthy, intelligent twenty-one-year-old college graduate, who has driven me crazy the last eighteen months with wedding lists, floral arrangements and choices of assorted hors d'oeuvres, has suddenly decided to spend this, the most important day of her life, locked in the Plaza Hotel john?

NORMA   (*Making her stand at the mantel*)   Yes! Yes! Yes! Yes! Yes!

ROY   (*Vicious*)   YOU MUSTA SAID SOMETHING! (*He storms into the bedroom.* NORMA *goes after him*)

NORMA   Roy . . . Roy . . . What are you going to do?

ROY   (*Stopping below the bed*)   First I'm getting the college graduate out of the bathroom! Then we're gonna have a wedding and then you and I are gonna have a big talk! (*He crosses to the bathroom door and pounds on it*) Mimsey! This is your father. I want you and your four-hundred-dollar wedding dress out of there in five seconds!

NORMA   (*Standing at the side of the bed*)   Don't threaten her. She'll never come out if you threaten her.

ROY   (*To* NORMA)   I got sixty-eight guests, nine waiters, four musicians and a boy with a wedding license waiting downstairs. This is no time to be diplomatic. (*Bangs on the door*) Mimsey! . . . Are you coming out or do we have the wedding in the bathroom?

NORMA Will you lower your voice! Everyone will hear us.

ROY (*To* NORMA) How long you think we can keep this a secret? As soon as that boy says "I do" and there's no one standing next to him, they're going to suspect something. (*He bangs on the door*) You can't stay in there forever, Mimsey. We only have the room until six o'clock . . . *You hear me?*
(*There is still no reply from the bathroom*)

NORMA Roy, will you please try to control yourself.

ROY (*With great display of patience, moves to the foot of the bed and sits*) All right, I'll stay here and control myself. You go downstairs and marry the short, skinny kid. (*Exploding*) *What's the matter with you?* Don't you realize what's happening?

NORMA (*Moving to him*) Yes. I realize what's happening. Our daughter is nervous, frightened and scared to death.

ROY Of what? OF WHAT? She's been screaming for two years if he doesn't ask her to marry him, she'll throw herself off the Guggenheim Museum . . . What is she scared of?

NORMA I don't know. Maybe she's had second thoughts about the whole thing.

ROY (*Getting up and moving to the bathroom door*) Second thoughts? This is no time to be having *second thoughts*. It's costing me eight thousand dollars for the *first* thoughts. (*He bangs on the door*) Mimsey, open this door.

NORMA Is that all you care about? What it's costing you? Aren't you concerned about your daughter's happiness?

ROY (*Moving back to her below the bed*) Yes! Yes, I'm concerned about my daughter's happiness. I'm also concerned about that boy waiting downstairs. A decent, respectable, intelligent young man . . . who I hope one day is going to teach that daughter of mine to grow up.

NORMA You haven't the faintest idea of what's going through her mind right now.

ROY Do you?

NORMA It could be anything. I don't know, maybe she thinks she's not good enough for him.

ROY (*Looks at her incredulously*) . . . Why? What is he? Some kind of Greek god? He's a plain kid, nothing . . . That's ridiculous. (*Moves back to the door and bangs on it*) Mimsey! Mimsey, open this door. (*He turns to* NORMA) Maybe she's not in there.

NORMA She's in there. (*Clutches her chest and sits on the side of the bed*) Oh, God, I think I'm having a heart attack.

ROY (*Listening at the door*) I don't hear a peep out of her. Is there a window in there? Maybe she tried something crazy.

NORMA (*Turning to him*) That's right. Tell a woman who's having a heart attack that her daughter jumped out the window.

ROY Take a look through the keyhole. I want to make sure she's in there.

NORMA She's in there, I tell you. Look at this, my hand keeps bouncing off my chest.
(*It does*)

ROY Are you gonna look in there and see if she's all right or am I gonna call the house detective?

NORMA (*Getting up and moving below the bed*) Why don't *you* look?

ROY Maybe she's taking a bath.

NORMA Two minutes before her own wedding?

ROY (*Crossing to her*) What wedding? She just called it off.

NORMA Wouldn't I have heard the water running?

ROY (*Making a swipe at her hat*) With that hat you couldn't hear Niagara Falls! . . . Are you going to look to see what your daughter's doing in the bathroom or do I ask a stranger?

NORMA (*Crossing to the door*) I'll look! I'll look! I'll look! (*Reluctantly she gets down on one knee and looks through the keyhole with one eye*) Oh, my God!

ROY What's the matter?

NORMA (*To him*) I ripped my stockings.
(*Getting up and examining her stocking*)

ROY Is she in there?

NORMA She's in there! She's in there! (*Hobbling to the far side of the bed and sitting down on the edge*)

Where am I going to get another pair of stockings now? How am I going to go to the wedding with torn stockings?

ROY (*Crossing to the bathroom*) If *she* doesn't show up, who's going to look at *you*? (*He kneels at the door and looks through the keyhole*) There she is. Sitting there and crying.

NORMA I *told* you she was in there . . . The only one in my family to have a daughter married in the Plaza and I have torn stockings.

ROY (*He is on his knees, his eye to the keyhole*) Mimsey, I can see you . . . Do you hear me? . . . Don't turn away from me when I'm talking to you.

NORMA Maybe I could run across to Bergdorf's. They have nice stockings.
(*Crosses to her purse on the bureau in the bedroom and looks through it*)

ROY (*Still through the keyhole*) Do you want me to break down the door, Mimsey, is that what you want? Because that's what I'm doing if you're not out of there in five seconds . . . Stop crying on your dress. Use the towel!

NORMA (*Crossing to* ROY *at the door*) I don't have any money. Give me four dollars, I'll be back in ten minutes.

ROY (*Gets up and moves below the bed*) In ten minutes she'll be a married woman, because I've had enough of this nonsnse. (*Yells in*) All right, Mimsey, stand in the shower because I'm breaking down the door.

NORMA (*Getting in front of the door*) Roy, don't get crazy.

ROY (*Preparing himself for a run at the door*) Get out of my way.

NORMA Roy, she'll come out. Just talk nicely to her.

ROY (*Waving her away*) We already had nice talking. Now we're gonna have door breaking. (*Through the door*) All right, Mimsey, I'm coming in!

NORMA No, Roy, don't! Don't!
(*She gets out of the way as* ROY *hurls his body, led by his shoulder, with full force against the door. It doesn't budge. He stays against the door silently a second; he doesn't react. Then he says calmly and softly*)

ROY Get a doctor.

NORMA (*Standing below the door*) I knew it. I knew it.

ROY (*Drawing back from the door*) Don't tell me I knew it, just get a doctor. (*Through the door*) I'm not coming in, Mimsey, because my arm is broken.

NORMA Let me see it. Can you move your fingers? (*Moves to him and examines his fingers*)

ROY (*Through the door*) Are you happy now? Your mother has torn stockings and your father has a broken arm. How much longer is this gonna go on?

NORMA (*Moving* ROY's *fingers*) It's not broken, you can move your fingers. Give me four dollars with your other hand, I have to get stockings.
(*She starts to go into his pockets. He slaps her hands away*)

ROY Are you crazy moving a broken arm?

NORMA Two dollars, I'll get a cheap pair.

ROY (*As though she were a lunatic*) I'm not carrying any cash today. Rented, everything is rented.

NORMA I can't rent stockings. Don't you even have a charge-plate?
    (*Starts to go through his pockets again*)

ROY (*Slaps her hands away. Then pointing dramatically*) Wait in the Green Room! You're no use to me here, go wait in the Green Room!

NORMA With torn stockings?

ROY Stand behind the rented potted plant. (*Takes her by the arm and leads her below the bed. Confidentially*) They're going to call from downstairs any second asking where the bride is. And *I'm* the one who's going to have to speak to them. *Me! Me! Me!* (*The phone rings. Pushing her toward the phone*) That's them. *You* speak to them!

NORMA What happened to *me me me?*
    (*The phone rings again*)

ROY (*Moving to the bathroom door*) Answer it. Answer it.
    (*The phone rings again*)

NORMA (*Moving to the phone*) What am I going to say to them?

ROY I don't know. Maybe something'll come to you as you're talking.

NORMA (*Picks the phone up*) Hello? . . . Oh, Mr. Eisler . . . Yes, it certainly is the big moment.
(*She forces a merry laugh*)

ROY Stall 'em. Stall 'em. Just keep stalling him. Whatever you do, stall 'em!
(*Turns to the door*)

NORMA (*On the phone*) Yes, we'll be down in two minutes.
(*Hangs up*)

ROY (*Turns back to her*) Are you crazy? What did you say that for? I told you to stall him.

NORMA I stalled him. You got two minutes. What do you want from me?

ROY (*Shakes his arm at her*) You always panic. The minute there's a little crisis, you always go to pieces and panic.

NORMA (*Shaking her arm back at him*) Don't wave your broken arm at me. Why don't you use it to get your daughter out of the bathroom?

ROY (*Very angry, kneeling to her on the bed*) I could say something to you now.

NORMA (*Confronting him, kneels in turn on the bed*) Then why don't you say it?

ROY Because it would lead to a fight. And I don't want to spoil this day for you. (*He gets up and crosses back to the bathroom door*) Mimsey, this is your father speaking . . . I think you know I'm not a violent man. I can be stern and strict, but I have never once been

violent. Except when I'm angry. And I am really angry now, Mimsey. You can ask your mother.
(*Moves away so* NORMA *can get to the door*)

NORMA (*Crossing to the bathroom door*) Mimsey, this is your mother speaking. It's true, darling, your father is very angry.

ROY (*Moving back to the door*) This is your father again, Mimsey. If you have a problem you want to discuss, unlock the door and we'll discuss it. I'm not going to ask you this again, Mimsey. I've reached the end of my patience. I'm gonna count to three . . . and by God, I'm warning you, young lady, by the time I've reached three . . . *this door better be open!*
(*Moving away to below the bed*) All right—One! . . . Two! . . . THREE! (*There is no reply or movement from behind the door.* ROY *helplessly sinks down on the foot of the bed*) . . . Where did we fail her?

NORMA (*Crosses to the far side of the bed, consoling him as she goes, and sits on the edge*) We didn't fail her.

ROY They're playing "Here Comes the Bride" downstairs and she's barricaded in a toilet—we must have failed her.

NORMA (*Sighs*) All right, if it makes you any happier, we failed her.

ROY You work and you dream and you hope and you save your whole life for this day, and in one click of a door, suddenly everything crumbles. Why? What's the answer?

NORMA It's not your fault, Roy. Stop blaming yourself.

ROY I'm not blaming myself. I know *I've* done my best.

Photo Credit: *Martha Swope*

Maureen Stapleton as Norma Hubley
George C. Scott as Roy Hubley
"Visitor From Forest Hills"

NORMA (*Turns and looks at him*) What does that mean?

ROY It means we're not perfect. We make mistakes, we're only human. I've done my best and we failed her.

NORMA Meaning *I* didn't do my best?

ROY (*Turning to her*) I didn't say that. I don't know what your best is. Only *you* know what your best is. Did you do your best?

NORMA Yes, I did my best.

ROY And I did my best.

NORMA Then we *both* did our best.

ROY So it's not our fault.

NORMA That's what I said before.
(*They turn away from each other. Then*)

ROY (*Softly*) Unless one of us didn't do our best.

NORMA (*Jumping up and moving away*) I don't want to discuss it any more.

ROY All right, then what are we going to do?

NORMA I'm having a heart attack, *you* come up with something.

ROY How? All right, I'll go down and tell them.
(*Gets up and moves to the bedroom door*)

NORMA (*Moving to the door in front of him*) Tell them? Tell them what?
(*As they move into the living room, she stops him above the sofa*)

ROY   I don't know. Those people down there deserve some kind of an explanation. They got all dressed up, didn't they?

NORMA   What are you going to say? You're going to tell them that my daughter is not going to marry their son and that she's locked herself in the bathroom?

ROY   What do you want me to do, start off with two good jokes? They're going to find out *some* time, aren't they?

NORMA   (*With great determination*)   I'll tell you what you're going to do. If she's not out of there in five minutes, we're going to go out the back door and move to Seattle, Washington! . . . You don't think I'll be able to show my face in this city again, do you? (ROY *ponders this for a moment, then reassures her with a pat on the arm. Slowly he turns and moves into the bedroom. Suddenly, he loses control and lets his anger get the best of him. He grabs up the chair from the dresser, and brandishing it above his head, he dashes for the bathroom door, not even detouring around the bed but rather crossing right over it.* NORMA *screams and chases after him*) ROY!
   (*At the bathroom door,* ROY *manages to stop himself in time from smashing the chair against the door, trembling with frustration and anger. Finally, exhausted, he puts the chair down below the door and straddles it, sitting leaning on the back.* NORMA *sinks into the bedroom armchair*)

ROY   . . . Would you believe it, last night I cried. Oh, yes. I turned my head into the pillow and lay there in the dark, crying, because today I was losing my little girl. Some stranger was coming and taking my little

Mimsey away from me . . . so I turned my back to you—and cried . . . Wait'll you hear what goes on *tonight!*

NORMA (*Lost in her own misery*) I should have invited your cousin Lillie. (*Gestures to the heavens*) She wished this on me, I know it. (*Suddenly* ROY *begins to chuckle.* NORMA *looks at him. He chuckles louder, although there is clearly no joy in his laughter*) Do you find something funny about this?

ROY Yes, I find something funny about this. I find it funny that I hired a photographer for three hundred dollars. I find it hysterical that the wedding pictures are going to be you and me in front of a locked bathroom! (*Gets up and puts the chair aside*) All right, I'm through sitting around waiting for that door to open.
(*He crosses to the bedroom window and tries to open it*)

NORMA (*Following after him*) What are you doing?

ROY What do you think I'm doing?
(*Finding it impossible to open it, he crosses to the living room and opens a window there. The curtains begin to blow in the breeze*)

NORMA (*Crosses after him*) If you're jumping, I'm going with you. You're not leaving *me* here alone.

ROY (*Looking out the window*) I'm gonna crawl out along that ledge and get in through the bathroom window.
(*He starts to climb out the window*)

NORMA Are you crazy? It's seven stories up. You'll kill yourself.

(*She grabs hold of him*)

ROY It's four steps, that's all. It's no problem, I'm telling you. Now will you let go of me.

NORMA (*Struggling to keep him from getting out the window*) Roy, no! Don't do this. We'll leave her in the bathroom. Let the hotel worry about her. Don't go out on the ledge.

(*In desperation, she grabs hold of one of the tails of his coat*)

ROY (*Half out the window, trying to get out as she holds onto his coat*) You're gonna rip my coat. Let go or you're gonna rip my coat. (*As he tries to pull away from her, his coat rips completely up the back, right up to the collar. He stops and slowly comes back into the room.* NORMA *has frozen in misery by the bedroom door after letting go of the coat.* ROY *draws himself up with great dignity and control. He slowly turns and moves into the bedroom, stopping by the bed. With great patience, he calls toward the bathroom*) Hey, you in there . . . Are you happy now? Your mother's got torn stockings and your father's got a rented ripped coat. Some wedding it's gonna be. (*Exploding, he crosses back to the open window in the living room*) Get out of my way!

NORMA (*Puts hand to her head*) I'm getting dizzy. I think I'm going to pass out.

ROY (*Getting her out of the way*) . . . You can pass out *after* the wedding . . . (*He goes out the window and onto the ledge*) Call room service. I want a double Scotch the minute I get back.

(*And he disappears from view as he moves across the ledge.* NORMA *runs into the bedroom and catches a glimpse of him as he passes the bedroom window, but then he disappears once more*)

NORMA (*Bemoaning her fate*) . . . He'll kill himself. He'll fall and kill himself, that's the way my luck's been going all day. (*She staggers away from the window and leans on the bureau*) I'm not going to look. I'll just wait until I hear a scream. (*The telephone rings and* NORMA *screams in fright*) Aggghhh! . . . I thought it was him . . . (*She crosses to the phone by the bed. The telephone rings again*) Oh, God, what am I going to say? (*She picks it up*) Hello? . . . Oh, Mr. Eisler. Yes, we're coming . . . My husband's getting Mimsey now . . . We'll be right down. Have some more hors d'oeuvres . . . Oh, thank you. It certainly *is* the happiest day of my life. (*She hangs up*) No, I'm going to tell him I've got a husband dangling over Fifty-ninth Street. (*As she crosses back to the opened window, a sudden torrent of rain begins to fall. As she gets to the window and sees it*) I knew it! I knew it! It had to happen . . . (*She gets closer to the window and tries to look out*) Are you all right, Roy? . . . Roy? (*There's no answer*) He's not all right, he fell. (*She staggers into the bedroom*) He fell, he fell, he fell, he fell . . . He's dead, I know it. (*She collapses onto the armchair*) He's laying there in a puddle in front of Trader Vic's . . . I'm passing out. This time I'm really passing out! (*And she passes out on the chair, legs and arms spread-eagled. The doorbell rings; she jumps right up*) I'm coming! I'm coming! Help me, whoever you are, help me! (*She rushes through the bedroom into the living room and to the front door)* Oh, please, somebody, help me, please!

> *(She opens the front door and* ROY *stands there dripping wet, fuming, exhausted and with clothes disheveled and his hair mussed)*

ROY *(Staggering into the room and weakly leaning on the mantelpiece. It takes a moment for him to catch his breath.* NORMA, *concerned, follows him)* She locked the window too. I had to climb in through a strange bedroom. There may be a lawsuit.

> *(He weakly charges back into the bedroom, followed by* NORMA, *who grabs his coattails in an effort to stop him. The rain outside stops)*

NORMA *(Stopping him below the bed)* Don't yell at her. Don't get her more upset.

ROY *(Turning back to her)* Don't get her *upset?* I'm hanging seven stories from a gargoyle in a pouring rain and you want me to worry about *her?* . . . You know what she's doing in there? She's playing with her false eyelashes. *(Moves to the bathroom door)* I'm out there fighting for my life with pigeons and she's playing with eyelashes . . . *(Crossing back to* NORMA*)* . . . I already made up my mind. The minute I get my hands on her, I'm gonna kill her. *(Moves back to the door)* Once I show them the wedding bills, no jury on earth would convict me . . . And if by some miracle she survives, let there be no talk of weddings . . . She can go into a convent. *(Slowly moving back to* NORMA *below the bed)* . . . Let her become a librarian with thick glasses and a pencil in her hair, I'm not paying for any more canceled weddings . . . *(Working himself up into a frenzy, he rushes to the*

table by the armchair and grabs up some newspapers)
Now get her out of there or I start to burn these
newspapers and smoke her out.

> *(NORMA stops him, soothes him, and manages to
> get him calmed down. She gently seats him on
> the foot of the bed)*

NORMA *(Really frightened)* I'll get her out! I'll get
her out! *(She crosses to the door and knocks)* Mimsey!
Mimsey, please! *(She knocks harder and harder)*
Mimsey, you want to destroy a family? You want a
scandal? You want a story in the *Daily News?* . . . Is
that what you want? Is it? . . . Open this door! *Open
it! (She bangs very hard, then stops and turns to* ROY*)*
. . . Promise you won't get hysterical.

ROY What did you do?
> *(Turns wearily to her)*

NORMA I broke my diamond ring.

ROY *(Letting the papers fall from his hand)* Your
good diamond ring?

NORMA How many do I have?

ROY *(Yells through the door)* Hey, you with the false
eyelashes! *(Getting up and moving to the door)* . . .
You want to see a broken diamond ring? You want to
see eighteen hundred dollars' worth of crushed ba-
guettes? . . . *(He grabs* NORMA's *hand and holds it to
the keyhole)* Here! Here! *This* is a worthless family
heirloom *(Kicks the door)*—and *this* is a diamond
bathroom door! *(Controlling himself. To* NORMA*)* Do
you know what I'm going to do now? Do you have
any idea? *(*NORMA *puts her hand to her mouth, afraid
to hear.* ROY *moves away from the door to the far side*

of the bed) I'm going to wash my hands of the entire Eisler-Hubley wedding. You can take all the Eislers and all the hors d'oeuvres and go to Central Park and have an eight-thousand-dollar picnic . . . *(Stops and turns back to* NORMA*)* I'm going down to the Oak Room with my broken arm, with my drenched rented ripped suit—and I'm gonna get blind! . . . I don't mean drunk, I mean totally blind . . . *(Erupting with great vehemence)* because I don't want to see you or your crazy daughter again, if I live to be a thousand.

> *(He turns and rushes from the bedroom, through the living room to the front door. As he tries to open it,* NORMA *catches up to him, grabs his tail coat and pulls him back into the room)*

NORMA   That's right. Run out on me. Run out on your daughter. Run out on everybody just when they need you.

ROY   You don't need me. You need a rhinoceros with a blowtorch—because no one else can get into that bathroom.

NORMA   *(With rising emotion)* I'll tell you who can get into that bathroom. Someone with love and understanding. Someone who cares about that poor kid who's going through some terrible decision now and needs help. Help that only *you* can give her and that *I* can give her. *That's* who can get into that bathroom now.

> *(*ROY *looks at her solemnly . . . Then he crosses past her, hesitates and looks back at her, and then goes into the bedroom and to the bathroom door.* NORMA *follows him back in. He turns and looks at* NORMA *again. Then he knocks gently on the door and speaks softly and with some tenderness)*

ROY Mimsey! . . . This is Daddy . . . Is something wrong, dear? . . . (*He looks back at* NORMA, *who nods encouragement, happy about his new turn in character. Then he turns back to the door*) . . . I want to help you, darling. Mother and I both do. But how can we help you if you won't talk to us? Mimsey can you hear me?

(*There is no answer. He looks back at* NORMA)

NORMA (*At the far side of the bed*) Maybe she's too choked up to talk.

ROY (*Through the door*) Mimsey, if you can hear me, knock twice for yes, once for no. (*There are two knocks on the door. They look at each other encouragingly*) Good. Good . . . Now, Mimsey, we want to ask you a very, very important question. Do you want to marry Borden or don't you?

(*They wait anxiously for the answer. We hear one knock, a pause, then another knock*)

NORMA (*Happily*) She said yes.

ROY (*Despondently*) She said no.

(*Moves away from the door to the foot of the bed*)

NORMA It was two knocks. Two knocks is yes. She wants to marry him.

ROY It wasn't a double knock "yes." It was two single "no" knocks. She doesn't want to marry him.

NORMA Don't tell me she doesn't want to marry him. I heard her distinctly knock "yes." She went (*Knocks twice on the foot of the bed*) "Yes, I want to marry him."

ROY It wasn't (*Knocks twice on the foot of the bed*) . . .
It was (*Knocks once on the foot of the bed*) . . . and
then another (*Knocks once more on the foot of the
bed*) . . . That's "no," twice, she's not marrying him.
(*Sinks down on the side of the bed*)

NORMA (*Crossing to the door*) Ask her again. (*Into the
door*) Mimsey, what did you say? Yes or no? (*They
listen. We hear two distinct loud knocks.* NORMA
turns to ROY) . . . All right? There it is in plain
English . . . You never *could* talk to your own
daughter.
(*Moves away from the door*)

ROY (*Getting up wearily and moving to the door*)
Mimsey, this is not a good way to have a conversation.
You're gonna hurt your knuckles . . . Won't you come
out and talk to us? . . . Mimsey?

NORMA (*Leads* ROY *gently to the foot of the bed*) Don't
you understand, it's probably something she can't
discuss with her father. There are times a daughter
wants to be alone with her mother. (*Sits* ROY *down
on the foot of the bed, and crosses back to the door*)
Mimsey, do you want me to come in there and talk
to you, just the two of us, sweetheart? Tell me, darling,
is that what you want? (*There is no reply. A strip of
toilet paper appears from under the bathroom door.*
ROY *notices it, pushes* NORMA *aside, bends down, picks
it up and reads it*) What? What does it say? (ROY
solemnly hands it to her. NORMA *reads it aloud*) "I
would rather talk to Daddy."
   (NORMA *is crushed. He looks at her sympa-
   thetically. We hear the bathroom door unlock.*
   ROY *doesn't quite know what to say to* NORMA. *He
   gives her a quick hug*)

ROY I—I'll try not to be too long.
(*He opens the door and goes in, closing it behind him, quietly.* NORMA, *still with the strip of paper in her hand, walks slowly and sadly to the foot of the bed and sits. She looks glumly down at the paper*)

NORMA (*Aloud*) . . . "I would rather talk to Daddy" . . . Did she have to write it on this kind of paper? (*She wads up the paper*) . . . Well—maybe I didn't do my best . . . I thought we had such a good relationship . . . Friends. Everyone thought we were friends, not mother and daughter . . . I tried to do everything right . . . I tried to teach her that there could be more than just love between a mother and daughter . . . There can be trust and respect and friendship and under-standing . . . (*Getting angry, she turns and yells toward the closed door*) Just because *I* don't speak to my mother doesn't mean *we* can't be different!
(*She wipes her eyes with the paper. The bathroom door opens. A solemn* ROY *steps out, and the door closes and locks behind him. He deliberately buttons his coat and crosses to the bedroom phone, wordlessly.* NORMA *has not taken her eyes off him. The pause seems interminable*)

ROY (*Into the phone*) The Green Room, please . . . Mr. Borden Eisler. Thank you.
(*He waits*)

NORMA (*Getting up from the bed*) . . . I'm gonna have to guess, is that it? . . . It's so bad you can't even tell me . . . Words can't form in your mouth, it's so hor-rible, right? . . . Come on, I'm a strong person, Roy. Tell me quickly, I'll get over it . . .

ROY (*Into the phone*) Borden? Mr. Hubley ... Can you come up to 719? ... Yes, now ... (*He hangs up and gestures for* NORMA *to follow him. He crosses into the living room and down to the ottoman where he sits.* NORMA *follows and stands waiting behind him. Finally*) She wanted to talk to me because she couldn't bear to say it to both of us at the same time ... The reason she's locked herself in the bathroom ... is she's afraid.

NORMA Afraid? What is she afraid of? That Borden doesn't love her?

ROY Not that Borden doesn't love her.

NORMA That she doesn't love Borden?

ROY Not that she doesn't love Borden.

NORMA Then what is she afraid of?

ROY ... She's afraid of what they're going to become.

NORMA I don't understand.

ROY Think about it.

NORMA (*Crossing above the sofa*) What's there to think about? What are they going to become? They love each other, they'll get married, they'll have children, they'll grow older, they'll become like us (*Comes the dawn. Stops by the side of the sofa and turns back to* ROY) —I never thought about that.

ROY Makes you stop and think, doesn't it?

NORMA I don't think we're so bad, do you? ... All right, so we yell and scream a little. So we fight and curse and aggravate each other. So you blame me for being a lousy mother and I accuse you of being a rotten husband. It doesn't mean we're not happy . . . does it? . . . (*Her voice rising*) Well? . . . Does it? . . .

ROY (*Looks at her*) . . . She wants something better. (*The doorbell rings. He crosses to open the door.* NORMA *follows*) Hello, Borden.

BORDEN (*Stepping into the room*) Hi.

NORMA Hello, darling.

ROY (*Gravely*) Borden, you're an intelligent young man, I'm not going to beat around the bush. We have a serious problem on our hands.

BORDEN How so?

ROY Mimsey—is worried. Worried about your future together. About the whole institution of marriage. We've tried to allay her fears, but obviously we haven't been a very good example. It seems you're the only one who can communicate with her. She's locked herself in the bathroom and is not coming out . . . It's up to you now.
(*Without a word,* BORDEN *crosses below the sofa and up to the bedroom, through the bedroom below the bed and right up to the bathroom door. He knocks*)

BORDEN Mimsey? . . . This is Borden . . . Cool it! (*Then he turns and crosses back to the living room. Crossing above the sofa, he passes the Hubleys, and without looking at them, says*) See you downstairs!
(*He exits without showing any more emotion. The Hubleys stare after him as he closes the door. But then the bathroom door opens and* NORMA *and* ROY *slowly turn to it as* MIMSEY, *a beautiful bride, in a formal wedding gown, with veil, comes out*)

MIMSEY I'm ready now!
>(NORMA *turns and moves into the bedroom toward her.* ROY *follows slowly, shaking his head in amazement*)

ROY *Now* you're ready? *Now* you come out?

NORMA (*Admiring* MIMSEY) Roy, please . . .

ROY (*Getting angry, leans toward her over the bed*) I break every bone in my body and you come out for "Cool it"?

NORMA (*Pushing* MIMSEY *toward* ROY) You're beautiful, darling. Walk with your father, I want to look at both of you.

ROY (*Fuming. As she takes his arm, to* NORMA) That's how he communicates? That's the brilliant understanding between two people? "Cool it"?

NORMA (*Gathering up* MIMSEY's *train as they move toward the living room*) Roy, don't start in.

ROY What kind of a person is that to let your daughter marry?
>(*They stop above the sofa.* MIMSEY *takes her bridal bouquet from the table behind the sofa, while* NORMA *puts on her wrap and takes her gloves from the back of the sofa*)

NORMA Roy, don't aggravate me. I'm warning you, don't spoil this day for me.

ROY Kids today don't care. Not like they did in my day.

NORMA Walk. Will you walk? In five minutes he'll marry one of the flower girls. Will you walk—
>(MIMSEY *takes* ROY *by the arm and they move to the door, as* NORMA *follows*)

ROY (*Turning back to* NORMA) Crazy. I must be out of my mind, a boy like that. (*Opens the door*) She was better off in the bathroom. You hear me? Better off in the bathroom . . . (*They are out the door . . .*)

Curtain